HAUNTED LENAWEE COUNTY

DR. JULIEANNA FROST

Published by Haunted America
A division of The History Press
An imprint of Arcadia Publishing
Charleston, SC
www.historypress.com

First published 2025

Manufactured in the United States

ISBN 9781467159326

Library of Congress Control Number: 2025937575

CONTENTS

PREFACE

I love a good story. As a professional historian, I have the honor of researching and teaching factual stories from the past as the work of my life. So it might seem unconventional that I have written a collection of legends of reputedly haunted places. However, a connection does exist between history and folklore. There are many instances of myths from the past being promoted as historical truth. I can still remember, as a child in grade school, learning the story of George Washington and his refusal to lie about injuring his father's cherry tree with a hatchet. It was taught to me as true, even when there was no historical evidence to this story. The tale first appeared in print in the fifth edition of the popular biography *The Life of George Washington* (1806). So why did my teacher tell me a tall tale? It could be that they did not realize the story was a myth. It could also be that they did not want the truth to get in the way of a good story. Although this tale was inaccurate, it imparted a cultural message about honesty. Many educators over the years promoted the idea that George Washington's success was directly connected to his good character. Our first president could thus serve as a good example for young children. By having such an honest role model, this story could help promote national pride.

Scary legends similarly may teach cultural lessons and serve other functions aside from catharsis. I recall my mother telling my sister and me about the bogeyman. Many cultures have variations of this type of spirit that punishes misbehaving children. My mom most often reminded us of the bogeyman when she wanted us to be quiet and go to sleep. She would say that if we were not good, the bogeyman would come and get us. This parenting technique did not help me to sleep, as I was terrified of the bogeyman, but it did make me silent. Likely, my mother had also been threatened by the bogeyman when she was little, as well as earlier generations of my English ancestors. So I am intrigued by the origin of legends and what might be gleaned from these tales, especially about the society that created and circulated them. What causes some to persist and others to disappear into the mists of time? What are the factual origins of these types of stories? What might they tell us about cultural fears and concerns of people over time? What could be learned from ghost stories?

American Studies Professor Linda S. Watts gave a good traditional definition of ghosts in the *Encyclopedia of American Folklore*: "Ghosts are the disembodied spirits of the dead. They are either the spirits of those who have recently died or those who have returned to travel among the living." She also noted that cemeteries and houses are popular locations for hauntings in folktales. Furthermore, sociologist Michael Mayerfeld Bell offers, in my opinion, a compelling modern argument for the existence of apparitions of the departed. In *The Ghosts of Place*, he wrote:

> *We moderns, despite our mechanistic and rationalistic ethos, live in landscapes filled with ghosts. The scenes we pass through each day are inhabited, possessed, by spirits we cannot see but whose presence we nevertheless experience.... Who has not experienced that flood of images of people long gone, or people when they were younger, while revisiting an old "haunt," as we say? Who has not had that slightly chilly, and yet very warm, feeling of almost being able to see your friends from when you were eight dashing down the sidewalk as you walk through the neighborhood where you grew up? Who has not had that sense, while creeping into some room where one really should not have been, that someone unseen was watching? Ghosts also help constitute the specificity of historical sites, of the places where we feel we belong and do not belong, of the boundaries of possession by which we assign ownership and nativeness.*

Ghosts are a near-universal social construct with variations depending on culture, time and place. Ghostly tales may serve functions like offering the hope of continued existence after death, warning of taboo behaviors, serving as social critiques or acting as a form of catharsis. I am very interested in the roots of hauntings. Why are some places considered haunted, while others are not? And how does the local community influence the specific characteristics of these alleged hauntings? As a historian, I cannot prove that ghosts exist. I can, however, prove that people believe that certain locations are haunted in Lenawee County.

I first began visiting Lenawee County, Michigan, in 1992. My future husband was born there, and we regularly visited with his family in Macon. Most of the stories I heard during that period were about the Frost and Murphy clans. I especially loved the humorous accounts of Aunt Naomi. Some of the early dates with my future spouse were also held in Lenawee County. I love to visit historic locations wherever I go and learn factual and fanciful details about them, and Lenawee County was no different. It was not until 2004, when I began to work at Siena Heights University, that I began to come across more local folklore, including ghost stories. A few years later, upon moving just seven miles from the northern border of Lenawee County and volunteering with community organizations, more and more legends came my way. I started an informal collection of these tales. When The History Press contacted me about a possible new project, I knew that the time was right to share these supernatural stories with a wider audience. I have only included legends that have been shared by the general public for several generations and that can be traced to actual verified historical events. So the A.K. Waldron house of Tecumseh is not included because of a report of a haunting from only one family. Likewise, the closed restaurant the Hathaway House of Blissfield lacks evidence of a woman rumored to have been strangled there. Perhaps the tales connected to those places will develop more over time. In the interim, I hope you enjoy this offering of *Haunted Lenawee County* and that it inspires you to go out and visit some of these sites to have your own encounters with the past.

ACKNOWLEDGEMENTS

This project would not have been possible without the advice, expertise and support of the following individuals and organizations: Elizabeth Artz, Dan Cherry, Lynn Frost, Marie Frost, Vanessa Gardner, Chuck Harpst, John Kuschell, Mike Mills, Bruce Neal, Mary Beth Reasoner, John Rodrigue, Pat Rowley, Lisa Schell, Sharon Scott, Stacy Tchorzynski, Bob Wessel, the Tecumseh Area Historical Museum, Tecumseh District Library, Cambridge Junction Historic State Park, Clinton Public Library, Clinton Historical Society, Lenawee County Historical Society, William G. Thompson Museum, Hudson Museum, Stair District Library, Village of Addison and Siena Heights University. This project has been a great joy. I am grateful to you all. This book is dedicated to my favorite ghouls: Erika, Laura, Liz and Vanessa.

CHAPTER 1
GHOST GIRL
ADDISON

The sudden death of a child must be one of the greatest heartbreaks. All the hopes and dreams that parents had for their offspring are gone in an instant. A ghost story from the village of Addison centers on such a loss. Reportedly, a young girl was waiting one morning for the school bus on North Adams Road. Even though this is a rural area, the traffic on this main route is often heavier at that time of day with people trying to get to work or school on time. One impatient commuter got stuck behind a slower-moving vehicle and decided to pass in a no-passing zone. In their hasty maneuver, they did not notice a schoolgirl standing on the side of the road at the end of her driveway. Though the reckless driver was able to pass a car, they hit the girl. She died at the scene.

Unlike a traditional apparition, this girl haunts several locations in the village of Addison. First, there is the location of her death on North Adams Road. In haunting folklore, a common theme is for the dead to dwell in a place that holds special significance to them, and the place of one's death would certainly be significant. In Addison, neighbors who live on the road where she lost her life sometimes hear a knocking on their doors, but when they open them, no one is there. Others say there are cold spots that manifest while walking near that location, even in the heat of summer.

Secondly, she is said to appear at the cemetery where she is buried. Hillside Cemetery, also known as the Addison Village Cemetery, dates back to 1834 with the village's founding. Overlooking the millpond below, it is a

This charming final resting place overlooking the Addison Mill Pond, Hillside Cemetery, dates to 1834. There are claims that the ghost of a little girl haunts this graveyard. *Author photo.*

beautiful resting place. There have been accounts of the ghost girl walking the grounds, seemingly oblivious to the fact that she is dead. In life, she loved colorful pinwheels, so fittingly, her grave has been decorated with one placed next to her tombstone. Visitors to her burial site have noticed the pinwheel spinning rapidly at times, even when there is no wind. This is taken as a sign of her presence. Cross-culturally, graveyards are common sites of paranormal experiences.

Finally, the family home of the schoolgirl has experienced strange phenomena since her passing. Lights flicker on and off. Knockings are heard with no apparent source. Perhaps most poignantly, in the backyard, her beloved swing set seems to have a mind of its own. Similar to the pinwheel, her favorite swing sways back and forth as if an invisible child is playing on it. The swinging might be a bittersweet comfort for the family, a visible sign that her soul persists.

This ghostly lore is atypical in that usually a spirit is connected to just one place, not flitting around and haunting many locations in a town. Perhaps this variation is because this anecdote has many of the elements of an urban legend. As Professor Linda Watts has defined this genre, "The tales are presented as true, and it is typical for the speaker to take pains to establish that they are true rather than merely a rumor or a hoax. The teller may believe the story is true because it goes through so many retellings that few realize that it is fiction. Urban legends usually forward a truth claim by including a believable premise." These narratives may be funny or spooky, and the details tend to change over time with greater embellishment. Maybe this is the reason why several places in the village are haunted by the ghost girl.

I wanted to verify what I could of the story of the ghost girl and perhaps track down her name. As of this writing, I have reviewed all of the recorded 851 burial records at the Hillside Cemetery. Taking into account that school buses were not instituted until the 1920s, this narrowed the field of graves that could be connected to the ghost girl. Only three girls would have been of the proper school age. I then reviewed their obituaries. One girl died in 1952 after an emergency appendectomy, one girl died in 1963 following a heart procedure and the final girl died in 2017 from a congenital defect. None of their stories match the details connected to the ghost girl story.

Even if this tale is not based in truth, that is not to say there is no value in the telling. Some of the obvious lessons include a caution to always follow the driving rules and to be aware of your surroundings. According to an NPR report, the Governors Highway Safety Association estimates that 7,500 pedestrians are killed by drivers every year. This ghost story also gives the hope that even death will not truly separate us from our loved ones, whether one believes in an afterlife or simply that our memory will continue to live on.

CHAPTER 2

SIENA HEIGHTS UNIVERSITY

ADRIAN

Siena Heights University is a private liberal arts university founded and sponsored in 1919 by the Adrian Dominican Sisters (ADS). Its main campus is located in the northeast of downtown Adrian on fifty-five acres. Next to the university is the campus for the ADS. The sisters initially started a Catholic boarding school for young women in 1896 called St. Joseph Academy. As the academy grew, Madden Hall, now the administrative building for the order, was built in 1911 to house these students. In 1919, the sisters expanded to create a Catholic liberal arts college for women, St. Joseph College, which initially shared a space with the academy. In 1939, to avoid confusion with two similarly named schools, St. Joseph College became Siena Heights College. In 1969, Siena Heights became coeducational and, in 1998, a university.

Currently, the student body of approximately 1,700 students can choose from over forty different programs of study and over twenty-five intercollegiate sports. Siena Heights University (SHU) was the first wireless campus in the state and has received several awards for its online programs. Some of the university's most popular programs include nursing, criminal justice, business and education. SHU might also be the most haunted institution of higher education in Lenawee County because several buildings are alleged to have ghosts.

The oldest campus building, Sacred Heart Hall, which opened in 1922, has been my home away from home as I worked there for over twenty years. Constructed in 1922 for then-named St. Joseph College, the structure blends

The beautiful Romanesque-style structure Sacred Heart Hall once served as the classroom space for St. Joseph College and St. Joseph Academy in Adrian. Several students have seen shadowy figures. *Author photo.*

Romanesque Revival and Neoclassical elements. It is almost impossible not to be impressed by the history of the place. As you walk through the main doors, you are greeted by an impressive double marble staircase with a statue of Jesus in the center foyer. Several large framed photos of the all-female classes from the 1960s and 1970s decorate the hall. This storied past is also highlighted by signs outside the rooms noting their earlier purposes. For example, my office area was the library reading room and reference area from the 1930s until 1956, and then from 1956 until 1972 it was a commuter lounge. In a way, it still served those purposes, as I liked to lounge when I was reading in the Division of the Humanities.

Two main areas of this structure are believed by some to be haunted. The fifth floor of the building, no longer in use, served as an art studio at one time. I toured the space once when a colleague somehow obtained a key to check it out. It was an extremely cramped space, more like a small attic annex than an appropriate studio. Some have reported scents wafting out from behind the door, such as paint or flowers. Sounds of movement have also been heard coming from the studio. At night, students walking across campus have noticed the lights flashing on and off both on the fourth and fifth floors, and a figure has been spotted staring out a fifth-floor window many times. Those who believe this to be a ghost have speculated that it is the spirit of Sister Jeannine Klemm. She became head of the Art Department in 1957 and found the fifth-floor studio to be inadequate. She spearheaded the fundraising effort for a new modern building, Studio Angelico, completed in 1969.

Another purported ghostly hot spot is the current library in Sacred Heart Hall. This two-story library was part of a 1955 addition to the hall and not original to the building, but it has the most reports of paranormal activity. The alleged spirit among the stacks is quite mischievous. Students have reported books flying off the shelves, cold spots and ghostly moans and footsteps. Librarians over the years have opened the library in the morning to find windows that had been closed the night before now opened, chairs pulled out from their normal places and books from the first floor relocated to the "Q" section of the Science area. Some have theorized that this spirit is of an Adrian Dominican sister or perhaps a novice who committed suicide. The story of a sister taking her own life has not been confirmed by historical sources. Sisters served as all of the faculty and staff at Siena Heights for generations until the shift to lay educators and staff that began in the 1970s. In her history of the school, Jennifer Hamlin Church noted, "In the aftermath of Vatican II, sisters had more mission options, and many chose health care or social work instead of teaching." Additionally, there began a decline in the number of women entering into religious orders.

Not surprisingly, many of the specters reported all across campus are thought to be the spirits of deceased sisters. The recent proliferation of religious workers featured in horror films, such as *The Nun* (2018), *Veronica* (2017) and *The Conjuring II* (2016), might be an influence on this belief. Shadows, cold spots and strange noises manifest in St. Dominic Chapel are thought to be the phantoms of Adrian Dominicans. The spirit of a reportedly murdered sister walks the basement area of the Motherhouse screaming, though it should be noted that steam heating does make some unusual sounds. However, I still would not want to wander the lower-ground floor areas alone, as I find the atmosphere quite spooky. Professor Peggy McCann had a student in 2015 show her a picture he had taken in one of the underground tunnels. She reported, "There's supposedly a nun that haunts the area, and he actually showed me a picture because he saw it and it looked as real as can be. It freaked me out a little bit because usually when there are places associated with nuns like Siena Heights, these stories and rumors pop up, but I really never believed it. It [a form] was up in the air hanging. It didn't look staged, Photoshopped or anything like that."

Now called Madden Hall, this building in Adrian opened in 1896 and initially served as St. Joseph Academy, an educational institution for young women. *Author photo.*

In addition, spirits have been spotted in the cemeteries that are adjacent to campus. The location of four cemeteries next door probably helps to encourage the spooky vibe. Oakwood Cemetery, founded in 1848, is located at 333 East Siena Heights Drive and has a gorgeous parklike setting of 120 acres. It is a good example of a Victorian garden cemetery with its elaborate monuments. Located across the street from Oakwood are St. Joseph's Catholic Cemetery and St. John's Lutheran Cemetery. These two small graveyards are adjacent to each other and well maintained. Finally, there is the Adrian Dominican Sisters Cemetery located behind the ADS campus. Some of my students found it brave when I went for a stroll in one of these cemeteries to take a break from grading, and some have asked me how I am not afraid to go into a graveyard. I tell them that in my experience, I have had more trouble with living people than the dead.

There have been many incidents reported in the residence halls, including lights and televisions turning on by themselves, toilets flushing with no one around, a figure of a sister standing over a student's bed one night, students being scratched by unknown assailants and the sound of disembodied voices, from whispers to bloodcurdling screams. The most infamous and widely shared ghostly tale at SHU focuses on the oldest section of the Archangeles residence hall. This spirit is perhaps the most unnerving. Beginning in the 1970s, room 211 had reports of doors opening and closing on their own, a rocking chair that would rock violently by itself and two points of unexplained light on a wall. The source for the light could not be determined, and attempts to paint over the phenomenon failed. Some thought that it was the spirit of a student who committed suicide. As room numbers have been updated over the years, no one is certain which room is 211, and some claim that room was permanently placed off-limits for the future housing of students. Oddly, the classroom buildings have few ghostly legends; there is only a phantom janitor who continues to push his cleaning cart through Studio Angelico.

Finally, in our most haunted campus tour there are two sites that no longer exist but I still think it important to note these legends for posterity's

The oldest section of the Ledwidge Residence Hall Complex, Archangeles Hall, opened in 1938 in Adrian. The following year, St. Joseph College was renamed Siena Heights. *Author's collection.*

sake. Before renovations of the Performing Arts Center, the old theater was said to have a young boy spirit that died during construction of the original building, but he has not yet manifested in the new theater. Sage Union Hall was demolished in 2018 due to its decline and inadequate funding to save it. It was the second-oldest building, opening as Walsh Hall in 1925. It initially housed the gymnasium and auditorium. Musical and theatrical events were regular occurrences at Walsh. In 1972, the building received the new name of Sage Union Hall. During my tenure, Sage Union housed the student center, including student organization offices, Upward Bound and the International Student office, as well as a nice café. Some of the unusual experiences of students and staff at this location include the sound of footsteps and whispers of unknown origin that were often heard in that building, the whistling of an unknown tune by an unknown entity and the feeling of being watched. In addition, an older couple was said to haunt the theater seats in the union. A former student shared, "If all the seats were put up at night, in the morning two seats in the front row would be down." It was a sad day for many when Sage Union was razed to the ground. Now in its place is a historical marker and an open lawn where students can be seen lounging and socializing. Even with the loss of these two buildings, I think I can still safely assert that SHU is the most ghostly institution of higher education in Lenawee County.

CHAPTER 3

ADRIAN COLLEGE

ADRIAN

Adrian College is a private liberal arts college in the United Methodist tradition with approximately 1,800 undergraduate and graduate students. Its one-hundred-acre campus is located centrally in the city of Adrian and offers over ninety pre-professional programs and majors. Currently, some of this institution's most popular majors include biology, marketing and sports management. Students are given the opportunity to take part in traditional athletics but also sports atypical for such a small school, such as ice hockey, esports, bass fishing, rowing, equestrian, cornhole and synchronized skating. The campus is very modern with state-of-the-art facilities.

So it is appropriate that the alleged haunted location on Adrian College's campus is its oldest surviving building, Downs Hall. Adrian College itself is the oldest surviving institution of higher education in the county; it was chartered as a college in 1859. Its roots are a bit older, as it began as a Wesleyan Methodist theological institute in Leoni, in Jackson County, in 1845. An MLive article described, "Between 1845 and 1848, five structures were built, including an assembly hall, chapel, and two women's dormitories. The most impressive structure was the men's residence hall. The three-story, brick building featured 48 rooms, each equipped with a flat-top stove and chimney." By 1855, this school had changed its name to Michigan Union College and enrolled approximately two hundred male and female students. Though the future initially looked bright for the institution, a lack of growth in the region convinced the trustees that they needed a more bustling location if the school was to survive. In addition, it was rumored that the Leoni area was not friendly toward the temperance stance of the college.

Adrian was selected and Dr. Asa Mahan, the former president of Oberlin College in Ohio, theologian, educator and ardent abolitionist, became Adrian College's first president. Of his tenure, he reminisced the following in his autobiography: "No single year passed under my presidency without one or more revivals of great power among the students, very frequently when no such work of grace existed within hearing distance around us."

In addition to the liberal arts college, the campus had a preparatory school, a theological school and a music conservatory. Campus buildings in the nineteenth century included the chapel (also called Downs Hall), Science Hall, North Hall, South Hall and Metcalf Hall. Only Downs Hall, built in 1860 in the Italianate style, still stands. This building houses the performing arts department, art gallery and student theater. Italianate architecture became commonplace between 1840 and 1885 with features like a multistory structure; overhanging eaves with decorative brackets, elaborately crowned; tall, arched windows; and a low-pitched roof, often with a square cupola on top.

Both of the ghostly tales take place in the theater. The first account references the building when it served as the chapel. It was not uncommon for children to be abandoned at religious institutions to be cared for there. A

This Italianate building, Downs Hall, is the only surviving structure of the original campus of Adrian College. Constructed in 1861, it originally served as the chapel. *Author's collection.*

young boy allegedly was dropped off in this manner at Downs Hall. Though the community provided for him to the best of their abilities, the abandoned child got sick and died. Some students believe that he haunts the theater. Former theater student Rosemary Regan shared that this spirit is mean and likes to play tricks on people. She related that once when she was painting the floor black backstage, she ran out of paint and so went to the storage area to get more. She distinctly remembered placing her paint roller in the paint tray and placing the stirrer next to the tray, but when she returned, the stirrer was in the tray. It would have been possible for an orphaned child to have been taken in at the college, but so far no corroborating sources have been uncovered as proof.

The second ghost story reports of a Confederate soldier who also met his demise in the chapel. He reportedly had left his regiment in order to find one of his enslaved persons who had run away. The soldier tracked his prey to Adrian, chasing after him into the chapel and following close behind as they ran up the right side of the staircase. The Confederate was either pushed or tripped and fell on his own bayonet. He bled out at the bottom of the stairs. People have reported seeing his apparition and believe they have heard his ghostly footsteps. Superstitious students still avoid the staircase where he theoretically died. This tale is certainly more exciting than that of the orphan but even less historically plausible.

The punishment for deserters during the Civil War (1861–65) was execution, usually by hanging or death by firing squad. Of particular pertinence to the ghostly Confederate story, the Confederate *Articles of War* (1861) specified that "all officers and soldiers who have received pay, or have been duly enlisted in the services of the Confederate States, and shall be convicted of having deserted the same, shall suffer death, or such other punishment as, by sentence of a court-martial, shall be inflicted." It seems like quite a risk to take to desert your men in order to search for your "property." After the loss at the Battle of Gettysburg (July 1–3, 1863), Confederate President Jefferson Davis offered leniency to deserters in an attempt to replenish the dwindling ranks, but the tide had already turned in favor of the Union. It would have been more logical for the soldier to have hired a professional slave catcher.

I think that there are several historical influences on the creation of this legend. First, Adrian College was well known for its abolitionist stance as a Wesleyan institution. This abolitionist sentiment led to the Wesleyan Methodist denomination being formed in 1841 due to a split from the Methodist Episcopal Church over church governance and the issue of

This interior view of Downs Hall of Adrian College shows the stage. Theatrical performances, art exhibits and musical recitals are regularly held in this former chapel. *Author's collection.*

slavery. To Wesleyans, slavery was a horrible institution that could not be tolerated by people of faith. President Mahan was a founding member of the Ohio Anti-Slavery Society, and he worked with other abolitionists. Lenawee County had formed the first antislavery society in the state, and activists such as Prior Foster, Elizabeth Comstock and Elizabeth Chandler worked to abolish slavery.

When Mahan lived in Adrian, he formed a friendship with Laura Smith Haviland, locally known as Aunt Laura, who was a conductor on the Underground Railroad. There are verified accounts of slave catchers coming north to capture fugitives. In her autobiography, Haviland told of the successful protection of the Hamilton family, who had escaped bondage, by the citizens of Adrian:

> *The citizens of Adrian appointed a meeting at the court-house, and sent for me to again tell the story of the slaveholder who had deeply laid his plans to capture, not only his fugitive slave Elsie and her four children, but also her husband, who was a free man. Other meetings were called to take measures for securing the safety of the hunted family from the iron grasp of the oppressor, whose arm is ever strong and powerful in the cause of evil; and so great was public excitement that the chivalrous sons of the South found*

Theologian Asa Mahan (1799–1889) served as the president of Oberlin College before he took on the same role at Adrian College. *Lenawee Historical Society.*

> *our Northern climate too warm for their constitutions, and betook themselves to the milder climate of Tennessee with as great speed as their hunted slave, with her husband, hastened away from there fifteen years before.*

There were other important instances of communities in Michigan coming together to thwart human traffickers, such as the Crosswhite case in Marshall, the Kentucky Raid in Cass County or the Cromwell case in Detroit.

Mahan and Haviland worked together on other social causes like petitioning the state to fund an orphanage. Aunt Laura had taken in orphans for much of her life, particularly connected to her interracial school, the Raisin Institute. After the Civil War, the Freedmen's Aid Society helped to run the school as an orphanage for Black children. It was a struggle to keep the school open. In 1871, the state agreed to support an orphanage, and in 1874, it was opened in Coldwater.

I believe that another influence on this ghost story is the direct support offered by Adrian College to the Union. In early 1861, the college offered its campus to serve as a training grounds for the Michigan Fourth Volunteer

Infantry. The city also raised funds to construct a mess and dining hall. The historical marker on Adrian's campus in part reads:

> *By early June ten companies of the Fourth had arrived and started their training. The 1,025 soldiers came from Adrian, Ann Arbor, Dexter, Jonesville, Hudson, Sturgis, Monroe, Hillsdale, Tecumseh, and Trenton. On June 21 nearly 30,000 people came to town to see the Fourth depart for Washington. The ladies of Adrian presented Colonel Dwight Woodbury with the regimental flag. Sewn into the flag was "The Ladies of Adrian to the Fourth Regiment Defend It."*

I theorize that given Adrian College's connections to abolitionism and the Civil War, it was fertile ground for a story about a Confederate soldier who met a bloody end and whose spirit can never rest. This story is a good example of how the historical events of a community can shape local folklore.

CHAPTER 4

THE GHOST TRESTLE

ADRIAN

Several areas of the United States have haunted tales connected to railroads. Some stories focus on ghost trains, nonhuman entities that for all eternity travel the same doomed route over and over. Perhaps most well known is the funeral train of Abraham Lincoln that, according to legend, is seen traveling from Washington, D.C., to Springfield, Illinois, around the anniversary of his assassination. The Association of American Railroads commented on this phenomenon: "The legend of the ghost train has its roots in the early days of steam locomotives and railway systems, a time when the sights and sounds of these powerful machines were still novel and frightening to the general public. Although ghost trains have been sighted throughout the world, the United States has its fair share of legends." There have been sightings of ghost trains in places such as Baton Rouge, Louisiana; Iredell County, North Carolina; and Marshall Pass, Colorado.

Another railroad structure that has inspired many a spooky narrative is the tunnel. Ghost tunnels exist in locations such as Moonville, Ohio; Richmond, Virginia; and North Adams, Massachusetts. In many instances, the structure is haunted either by workers who were killed by accidents during its construction or passengers who died during a horrible train wreck.

Correspondingly, another structure has spawned similar tales: the railroad bridge trestle. Some examples of haunted trestles are those located near Stillwater, Minnesota; Avon, Indiana; and Adrian, Michigan. The last railroad bridge mentioned is located in Madison Township, near the city and northeast of the town of Sand Creek. People claim to have had strange

Covered in graffiti, this trestle bridge southwest of Adrian is where many teenagers have proved their bravery by visiting it at night with friends. *Author photo.*

experiences at the graffiti-covered structure. Some have heard disembodied cries and others a phantasmic male voice shouting a warning. Individuals have also reported the malfunctioning of batteries of all types at the site. Cellphones, cameras, flashlights and car batteries have mysteriously gone dead, with spirits being blamed for this electrical sabotage. There are even those who claim that if you sprinkle flour thickly across your windshield, spectral handprints will eerily appear in the powder like a ghostly science experiment.

The ghost trestle has a few different legends connected to it, with several variations as to why the place is haunted. The most widespread story is that a farm was located near the trestle, which crosses over Bailey Highway, south of Gier Road. A family of three lived there: a husband, a wife and an infant child. One fateful day, the barn on the property caught fire. The father frantically attempted to put out the fire, while the mother with her child ran toward the train tracks in an attempt to wave down a passing train for assistance. Unfortunately, all in the family would perish on that day. The fire consumed the farmer and spread to also destroy the house. His wife and

After the unmarked burial site of victims of the Wabash disaster was found in 2016 in the Oakwood Cemetery of Adrian, the Italian Consul in Detroit raised funds to commission this memorial by Sergio De Giusti. *Author photo.*

child were hit and killed by the train when they slipped near the tracks in their desperate search for help. There is no historical corroboration for this event, so let us hope that this very unlucky family never existed at all.

Another tale also has a fire at a house near the trestle as a central feature. According to Dr. Robert Wessel, one of the tireless volunteers of the Lenawee Historical Society, "It was the home of a family with three daughters, all under the age of twelve. It is said that the parents and two daughters died in the fire, and the third fell into the well and drowned while trying to escape." No historical evidence has yet been found to support this story, either.

The final legend does, however, have its roots in a well-documented historical event, the 1901 wreck of the Wabash Railroad. On Thanksgiving eve, around 6:46 p.m., the No. 13 westbound train and No. 4 eastbound train struck each other head-on between Seneca and Sand Creek. On November 28, 1901, the *Detroit Free Press* reported, "On train No. 13 the scenes were sickening. The first two coaches were filled with emigrants, part of whom were asleep. The crash was terrible and the cars were piled upon each other, and taking fire, the confusion was terrible. The shouts and cries for help went up and appalled all who were near, and who were helpless. Hotter and hotter grew the flames, as if in anger, and more heartrending were the piercing shrieks for help." The horrific accident claimed an estimated one hundred lives, reducing some bodies to ashes. Historian Dr. Laurie Perkins highlighted that many of those on the eastbound train were heading home to Thanksgiving gatherings, and many on the westbound train were Italian immigrants hoping for a better future by getting work in the coal mines in Trinidad, Colorado. Though the location of the wreck of the Wabash is some distance from the ghost trestle, some believe these lost souls haunt the area.

Another legend that has sprung from this tragedy is that a mother trapped inside one of the burning cars tossed her infant child out of a window to safety, while she perished in the flames. Her spirit now wanders the tracks looking for her child.

Regardless of which of these ghost stories one prefers, I find it interesting that the motif of home is featured in each, whether it is the ultimate loss set in motion by a house fire or a transportation accident that prohibits the return to home or the ability to find a new one. Ideally, home is where we are safe and loved, and this is often reflected in the tales we tell.

Chapter 5

The Mineral Springs Hotel

Adrian

On West Maumee Street, an impressive building still has a sign on its front that reads "W. Maumee Trading Co." from when it operated as an antique store many years ago. This property located in Adrian has had several incarnations as a business and during its history had connections to multiple catastrophes. In part due to the springs on the property, the first business was a beer garden. German immigrants brought their social drinking traditions with them to Adrian, and by the late nineteenth century, several beer gardens and breweries were in operation. Joseph Pfeiffer was one such immigrant from Württemberg. On January 1, 1859, he married fellow German immigrant Caroline Myers. In that same year, Pfeiffer formed a partnership with fellow compatriot William Lehman and established the Brick Brewery, later renamed the Union Brewery. Within about seven years, Pfeiffer would sell his interest and in 1866 purchase a beer garden located at Maumee and Race Streets, along the south branch of the River Raisin. According to historian Charles Lindquist, Pfeiffer began renovations in 1871 such as boring an artesian spring well and adding a third floor to the brick building the following year. The Pfeiffers opened it as the Mineral Springs Hotel circa 1873 with accommodations for forty-four guests. The *General History of the State of Michigan* noted, "The Mineral Springs, connected with the hotel by that name, located in the western part of the paved district, are pronounced by chemists, and shown by analysis, to be possessed of excellent medicinal properties. They are well patronized, with the best results. The bath and hotel accommodations are of the first order." In addition, the hotel continued to operate its own beer garden.

The nineteenth century saw the growth in popularity of hot springs and mineral springs resorts, such as the Mineral Springs Hotel of Adrian. Some paranormal investigators theorize that mineral springs especially amplify ghostly activity. *Author photo.*

Mineral water spa resorts provided popular treatments across the United States in the early nineteenth century. In his study, Loring Bullard noted that "after the Civil War, efforts to describe and classify mineral springs and use systematic methods to discern their therapeutics intensified. Spa doctors, by then, had reached general agreement that mineral waters primarily helped chronic ailments, such as rheumatism, gout, dyspepsia, and scrofula." Patients at places like the Mineral Springs Hotel were "taking the waters" in an attempt to heal themselves. Water treatments could consist of drinking the water or bathing in the water. Not surprisingly, since many of the people who visited spas like this were very ill, some would never check out. For example, John Born passed away at the hotel on June 30, 1877. Financially, the Mineral Springs Hotel was able to profit from its natural springs and was a popular destination. Unfortunately, the proprietor Joseph Pfeiffer unexpectedly died within three years of opening on August 24, 1876, of typhoid fever at age sixty-one. His widow, Caroline, took over the operations of the hotel to support herself. She would be at the helm of the Mineral Springs Hotel during one of the greatest disasters to befall the city on October 2, 1879.

As I discussed in my previous book on Adrian, the Lenawee County Fair was held in the city beginning in 1839. The original fairgrounds were located downtown. The County Agricultural Society, unfortunately, fell on hard economic times, and the fairground property was sold as a foreclosure. Local businessman Willis T. Lawrence purchased it and agreed to rent it to the society for their annual county exhibition. He reportedly put $18,000 of his own money into improving and enlarging the fairgrounds. The *Detroit Free Press* on October 4, 1879, imparted, "He gave special attention to the landscape effects, and had in view a design of making 'Lawrence Park' one of the most beautiful race-courses and exhibition grounds in the country." Included in these improvements was a large grandstand with an alleged capacity for two thousand people. The *Detroit Free Press* described what happened during the premiere performance in front of the new structure filled with spectators.

> *The band was playing a lively air and no one heard the first sharp snap of the breaking structure. But for all that no one that happened to be there mistook the indescribable sensation of falling. In the twinkling of an eye the music stopped and the sound of crashing timbers, the screams of the struggling victims and the exclamations of the appalled spectators filled the air. Occupants of dwellings a mile distant heard the horrifying sound and comprehended that a fatal catastrophe had happened.*

Historian Charles Lindquist put the death toll at approximately twenty people, with hundreds more suffering serious injuries.

Due to the proximity to the disaster site, the Mineral Springs Hotel and the Croswell Opera House both served as makeshift hospitals for the injured. There were many broken bones, internal injuries and open wounds. Town doctors and physicians from the surrounding area rushed to help, but for some, the efforts were in vain. For example, Daniel Johnson of Dover, Michigan, was immediately taken across the way to the hotel to be treated but passed away. Several people would be charged with manslaughter, including owner Lawrence, the architect and the builders.

The next year, another person would lose their life near the hotel. Two men got into an altercation one evening at the inn. The nightwatchman, Dennis Lyon, was notified to help break up the fight. The *Detroit Free Press* reported, "Lyon was called and started to arrest Aiken, who ran, and as Lyon followed, turned and fired a pistol, the ball entering Lyon's head just above the eye and passing through, killing him instantly. Aiken in the

The 1879 tragedy bankrupted the Lenawee County Fair, but in 1884, a new site in Adrian was purchased, and this agricultural tradition continues today. *Author's collection.*

confusion escaped." It is uncertain if Frank Aiken was ever brought to justice for his crime.

Caroline Pfeiffer continued to operate the Mineral Springs Hotel until 1894, when she defaulted on a loan and the hotel was put up at a tax sale auction. Unfortunately, she was committed to the Kalamazoo Asylum for the Insane that same year. Her diagnosis is unknown, but it was reported that she had been suffering for several years and that she had been under severe financial stress in running the hotel since her husband's death. Though the Kalazazoo Asylum was viewed as progressive in its treatment of mental illness, one can imagine the distress that Caroline encountered during her confinement. A severe critique of the institution was written by former patient Lydia Smith, who spent four years there after her husband had her involuntarily confined so he could have a relationship with another woman. She commented, "I have thought many a time that I would willingly give my life, if by so doing I could save a soul from a life from eternal woe. And I would willingly give the remainder of my life if by so doing I could save one soul from suffering what I have suffered at the Kalamazoo Asylum." Caroline would spend the rest of her days at the asylum until her death at the age of seventy-nine in 1902 from heart failure.

As mineral springs resorts had fallen out of fashion by the turn of the century, the Mineral Springs Hotel building was sold in 1903, and the property served other purposes. For example, it served as headquarters for the Citizen's Light and Power Company until 1941. Other businesses in this location over the years have included a tire shop, an appliance store and, when I first moved to the area, an antique store. Those who have had supernatural experiences at this location, however, believe the phenomenon is connected to the events that happened when it was a hotel.

People have reported hearing disembodied male and female voices and banging on the walls, feeling sudden cold spots and even seeing full-bodied apparitions. Paranormal investigator Jeff Westover, in his *Ghost Highway* blog, told a tale about a former owner.

> *John related to me a story about his wife Kristen (now deceased) whose wedding ring went missing inside the store. They looked everywhere, including examining every piece of trash in the dumpster outside, but could not find the ring. Days later, Kristen was climbing the stairway between the first and second floor when a bright flash of light was directed at her eye. It was the missing ring sitting at the top of the stairway, perfectly refracting the morning sunlight directly toward her eyes. Those stairs were climbed hundreds of times between the ring's disappearance and reappearance.... It would've been found had it been there the entire time. Kristen's daughter, Molly, verified the story.*

Several paranormal groups have investigated this site and believe the water at the location and the electrical substation nearby may amplify the energy of the spirits. The top two floors of the building show evidence of its former use, with peeling wallpaper and antique fixtures from another time. We can imagine the lives of those who once passed through the Mineral Springs Hotel. The last business located here closed several years ago, and the property is awaiting a new venture to breathe life into this historic structure.

CHAPTER 6

CROSWELL OPERA HOUSE

ADRIAN

For over 150 years, people have been enthralled with tales of comedy and tragedy that have played out on the stage and screen of the Croswell Opera House in Adrian, Michigan. When I visit this beautiful space with its ornate plaster, lighting and decorative panels, I am immediately transported back in time. Many of my personal heroes spoke in this auditorium: Susan B. Anthony, Elizabeth Cady Stanton, Frederick Douglass, Ralph Waldo Emerson, Gloria Steinem, Bella Abzug, Ralph Nader and Julian Bond. So this place is hallowed ground for that reason alone for me. Then there are the personal memories of all the wonderful shows I have seen over the years. This grand theater was the brainchild of Charles Croswell, mayor of Adrian and former senator and governor of the great state of Michigan.

Croswell came from New York at the age of seven in 1837 to live with his maternal uncle Daniel Hicks, as the orphaned Croswell had lost his entire family—father, mother and sister. Croswell would eventually study law and form a law firm in 1855. He was very civic-minded and championed improvements for the state, such as election law reform, reduced public debt and establishment of the State House of Corrections and the Eastern Asylum for the Insane. Croswell was also instrumental in several improvements for the city of Adrian. One of these was the Adrian Union Hall, later to be called the Croswell Opera House. Croswell helped finance the project, and this theater, designed by Horatio Nelson White, came to fruition by 1866. This makes the Croswell Opera House one of the oldest theaters in the state and one of the oldest continuously operating theaters in the United States.

Over the decades, the theater hosted lectures, musical performances, plays and films. There were also various improvements and expansions to the building. For example, the 2017 article *Croswell 150 Years Old and Improved*, reported, "In May, when the building reopens after a year of extensive renovations, patrons will find plenty of changes at the venerable old theater: a new lobby, a new 'black box' performance space upstairs, a new venue for events in what was previously called the Heritage Room and more restrooms. Not to mention the new sound and lighting equipment and a number of other improvements less visible to theatergoers." The Croswell, even with recent innovations, most closely resembles the structure in the interior theater as it did in the 1920s. During the Roaring Twenties, the Croswell suffered strong competition from the new popular medium of motion pictures. Renovations were begun by Harry Angell and Robert Codd, who purchased the property in 1919, to update the business to resemble other movie palaces of the period. Film projection equipment and latticed towers for the pipe organ were added, as well as decorative plasterwork and a new horseshoe balcony by 1921.

Many of the purported hauntings are located in the balcony. People have reported seeing shadow people sitting in this location, and one is in the form of a little girl. Recall that, like the Mineral Springs Hotel, the Croswell Opera House was put into service as a makeshift hospital and morgue during the grandstand collapse disaster. Theater professor Mark DiPietro described, "Because when it was first built the theater had a flat floor—not raked, or slanted toward the stage, as it is today—and the seats weren't fixed to the floor and therefore could be removed completely, the building was pressed into service as a hospital for almost three weeks in 1879 when the grandstand at the fairgrounds, then located on Race Street collapsed. Out of the many injured who were treated at the Croswell, 14 people, including a little girl, died there." Some believe this is the little girl haunting the balcony.

Another shadow person that manifests in the balcony and other locations in the Croswell appears to be male. He wears a top hat, gloves and an overcoat. A former executive director and an artistic director of the Croswell both had separate encounters with the figure. It is theorized that perhaps it is the ghost of Charles Croswell. One can imagine Croswell, who later became the sole owner of the theater, might spend his afterlife in a place so dear to him. Another possible theory is that it is the spirit of Charles Croswell Jr. After his father purchased the theater, Charles Jr. was appointed manager of the opera house. He lost this position after his father died in 1886. While

The Croswell Opera House of Adrian is the oldest continuously operating theater in the state and one of the oldest in the United States. *Author photo.*

staying in Chicago, Charles Jr. took his own life in 1891. The *Detroit Free Press* reported, "Aged 30, son of the late ex-Governor Croswell, suicided with morphine in his room at a cheap hotel....The act is attributed to despondency, young Croswell having lived an unsettled existence for several years and being during the last few weeks without employment or money." The *True Republican* added, "Croswell was a very bright man and acted as his father's private secretary while the later was governor of Michigan. He was about 30 years old and for several years has lived a wandering existence. He seemed to be in hard luck financially."

Other apparitions are assumed to be unknown audience members or actors. The book *Behind the Curtain: 150 Years at Michigan's Oldest Theater* related the following:

> *Another story involves the cast of a high school show rehearsing on a Saturday morning. They had stopped the rehearsal to work on a scene and notice a group of people, all older adults, dressed like ushers in white shirts sitting in the balcony. The cast assumed there was a group touring the Croswell for some reason, and thought nothing of it, and then turned their attention to the director, but when they turned back to face the house barely more than a few seconds later, the group was gone.*

In another incident, Bob Soller, former artistic director, looked up at the catwalk late one night and noticed a light on. He went and turned it off. The light came back on, and once again he extinguished it. His efforts were in vain because when he returned to the stage, the bulb was glowing up above once again. Other unexplained experiences happened to costume manager Emily Gifford, who reported seeing a glimpse of a woman in a nineteenth-century red dress who seemed to like knocking stuff over in the costume storage area and then dematerializing. Gifford also heard male voices from the wings stage right while rehearsing with an actor, and when they went to investigate, they could find no other people in the theater. Finally, during a 1992 production of *Oliver* at the theater, two actors reported seeing a white figure float from one of the cabinets in the shop located in the basement. I personally know one of these actors, and I can attest that they are not prone to exagerration.

As is true for many of the places included in this collection, several paranormal investigators have visited the Croswell. In 2013, a ghost-hunting group called Friends Researching Entities and Known Spirits (FREAKS) conducted an examination of the theater. Their evidence included photographs of orbs, high EMF readings in certain locations of the theater and phrases picked up using an Ovilus, or "ghost box." As a historian, I find the most frightening story connected to the Croswell to be how close we came to losing this architectural and historical treasure. In 1967, the

The final resting place of Governor Charles Croswell (1825–1886) is located in Oakwood Cemetery of Adrian, though some believe that his ghost still haunts the Croswell Opera House. *Author photo.*

Butterfield movie chain that leased the theater resolved not to renew, and Harry Angell decided to sell the building. There was talk that the place would be demolished. Historian Charles Lindquist recounted:

> *In late 1967 a local amateur theater group was organized called the Croswell Opera House and Fine Arts Association and they decided to buy the property to convert it back into a theater for live plays, musicals, and lectures. Charles Hickman, the co-founder of Brazeway and the* [Hickman Family] *Foundation, was at the center of this group. Gaylord Baker and Catherine Smith were others, and so were Carlo Heikkinen, Adrian superintendent of schools, and Ray Maxe, Parks and Recreation director of the City of Adrian.*

This tale proves once again the adage that "not all heroes wear capes."

CHAPTER 7
DEAD MAN'S CURVE
CAMBRIDGE TOWNSHIP

A stretch of U.S. 12 in Lenawee County near Allen Lake has been called "Dead Man's Curve" for generations. Similarly to other U.S. roads given this label, an abrupt curve in the Irish Hills region has caused numerous fatalities. However, unlike those other roads, the "Dead Man's Curve" phrase here has an additional interpretation: some believe the accidents have been caused instead due to the location being cursed.

As a travel route, U.S. 12 has roots back to the Pleistocene era, when it was used as a path for migratory animals such as mastodons. Humans hunting such animals also used this trail, and over time, it became a major trade route for Native Americans from Canada through the territories of Michigan, Indiana and Illinois, ending at the Mississippi River. Later European settlers would call it the Old Sauk Trail or Great Sauk Trail, though it was used by several Indigenous peoples, not just the Sauk tribe.

In 1827, governmental funds were allocated to develop a westward military road that predominantly followed the Old Sauk Trail from Detroit to Chicago. This highway would also become known as the Chicago Road. To improve transportation and encourage immigration to the Michigan territory further, in 1828, a massive project was undertaken to make the Old Sauk Trail into a wagon road. Willis F. Dunbar and George S. May described:

> *These roads were a far cry from their modern counterparts. It can hardly be said that they were* built *at all, as we think of highway building today. Surveyors selected the route, often following Indian trails, axemen cut away*

> *the brush and felled trees low enough along the path so wagons could pass over the stumps, and workmen constructed crude bridges over streams which could not easily be forded. Logs were laid across the road over bogs and swamps to prevent wagons and animals from miring. This was known as a* corduroy road. *Other than this, little was done to provide a surface for the roads.*

One report of the Chicago Road described that it "stretches itself by devious and irregular windings east and west like a huge serpent lazily pursuing its onward course utterly unconcerned as to its destination." Even so, this road was still the quickest route, taking five days to travel between the cities of Detroit and Chicago during the stagecoach era. Two stagecoaches per week ran this throughway by 1835, and stagecoach stops lined the route approximately every twenty miles.

The Old Sauk Trail would see greater improvements with the proliferation of the automobile in the early twentieth century. The demand for a national highway system gained traction in 1912, and the Federal Highway Act passed in 1921. Federal money was available to create an interstate network of modern concrete highways. This aid encouraged an immense infrastructure program in the state of Michigan. Better roads also helped support the growth in the industry of automobile tourism. An advert in the *Ohio Motorist* of 1923 boldly encouraged, "Get acquainted with the free camping sites, the summer resorts, the lakes, the streams, the forests, and beautiful drives of Michigan…Vacation in Michigan. You will live longer to enjoy its memory." By 1923, improvement projects had begun on the route between Chicago and Detroit, then designated U.S. 12. Part of this plan was to straighten out the route in certain sections, including in the Irish Hills, which was quite meandering. On November 17, construction workers were excavating a knoll when they made an alarming discovery of human remains. So this part of the road was both a literal and figurative "dead man's curve."

To be specific, not only men but also women and children were buried at the gravesite between the years of 1760 and 1810. Nine skeletons were retrieved initially, along with several funerary artifacts. On November 20, 1923, the *Ironwood Daily Globe* reported, "The bones lay in the middle of the road and were dug up by a steam shovel which crushed and badly broke many of them."

The bodies and their funerary offerings were taken to a nearby home, while construction continued on the road. Before an anthropologist could even arrive from Ann Arbor, trophy hunters had robbed much of the

This photograph shows Dead Man's Curve, located in the Irish Hills region, looking west. This stretch of road has a notorious reputation for being the site of accidents. *Author photo.*

remains. Only a cranium of an individual estimated between the age of ten and fifteen years old and some objects survived the plunder. The Federal Register later reported the following state excavation and inventory of 1995 by Assistant Archaeologist Barbara Reed:

> *The state museum also cataloged a group of 18 funerary objects associated with the human remains disinterred during road construction in the 1920s. The 18 associated funerary objects are: One pewter spoon, one bottle, one oval stone, one deer mandible, three loose teeth, one lot of fur pieces with tassels wrapped in porcupine quill, one silver armband, one wooden bowl or toy canoe, one lot of wool scraps, one lot of linen scraps, one silver armband, one copper or brass kettle fragment, one iron knife blade, one lot of very small bone chips, one lot of shell and glass beads and one pewter bowl.*

The mass grave was presumed to have been likely from the Potawatomi culture.

In 1923, a legal case ensued to determine the appropriate custody of the remains. It was decided to rebury them in a nearby location to the original site. The site selected was the Walker Tavern, a tourist attraction, approximately five miles away at the crossroads of U.S. 12 and M-50. (The two Walker

Taverns will have their entry later in this book.) The proprietor, Reverend Frederick Hewitt, offered his property as a final resting place. This was accepted that same year, but for some unknown reason, the reinterment did not occur until 1925. On May 20, 1925, the *Battle Creek Enquirer* announced, "The public is invited to attend this ceremony which will duplicate as far as possible the funeral rites of the native Indians. A cairn will be built for which each person who attends is asked to bring a stone, this to be a memorial for the Indians." The service took place on Sunday afternoon, May 24. On May 29, the *Battle Creek Enquirer* further reported:

> *In the order of service, Mr. Hewitt (former pastor of a church in Marshall) read a passage of scripture, and L. Whitney gave "A Tribute to the Potawatamie Indians." The Lord's Prayer was given in unison and the Rev. Coudon gave the committal prayer and benediction. The procession that followed the antique rosewood casket that held the remains of some Indians, included the undertaker, clergy, speaker, and special Indian representatives, children with wildflowers, corn, beans, squash, boys with wild game according to ancient Indian customs, and members of the Lenawee Historical association.*

The Native American remains found at Dead Man's Curve were interred at Walker Tavern, then a roadside attraction at Cambridge Junction. This postcard shows the burial cairn. *Author's collection.*

Reverend Hewitt's sincerity in providing a dignified resting place might be considered suspect, however, because he displayed Native American artifacts in his attraction, publicized the grave and had an inaccurate sign placed in front of the burial cairn that read, "Here Lie the Remains of 9 Potawatomi Indians." A jaded person might believe Hewitt used the burial as another draw to his tourist trap. He advertised the Indian grave in his promotional literature.

After the road project was completed on U.S. 12, accidents that took place on the stretch of road near the disturbed grave were viewed by some locals as proof that the area was cursed by Native American spirits. It is possible that certain drivers would rather blame a hex than admit that they were driving poorly. Those that promoted the idea of the curse believed that unwary motorists were punished due to modern development violating a sacred Indian burial ground. This interpretation has its roots in the well-worn cliche from supernatural literature and films. The Indian burial ground trope consists of a haunting caused by white people disturbing sacred Indigenous land. Its reputed origin in print is Philip Freneau's poem "The Indian Burying Ground" (1787). Take the following section from this work:

Thou, stranger, that shalt come this way,
No fraud upon the dead commit—
Observe the swelling turf, and say
They do not lie, but here they sit.

Native American scholar Terri Jean, in *Digging Up the Indian Burial Ground Trope*, posits several reasons for the longevity of this narrative convention. Firstly, it was popular and so others copied it in their works. Second, it reinforces the even older trope of portraying Native Americans as evil with special powers. Third, due to great ignorance among the white population about Native Americans, such stereotypes can flourish. Fourth, the graves are unmarked and thus mysterious. Finally, white guilt or settler guilt could create an underlying fear that wronged Native Americans will one day seek violent retribution against those who displaced them. In many instances of these fictive and historical events of transgression, the departed were not treated with proper respect, and no thought was given to return the remains to their tribe for a proper burial with appropriate rites.

It would take many years before the passage of the Native American Graves Protection and Repatriation Act of 1990 (NAGPRA) began to address some of the wrongs of the past. This act outlined the process by which museums and federal agencies are required to return Native American artifacts and human remains to their descendants or tribes. Over the years prior, the cairn and the wooden Walker Tavern had fallen into disrepair. In 1965, the State of Michigan purchased eighty acres of the property and developed it as a professional museum, which includes the Hewitt House, original Walker Tavern and Barn. The cairn was removed, and the burial site was not advertised as an attraction any longer. In compliance with the NAGPRA, in 2018 the Michigan State Historic Preservation Office decided that "there is a relationship of shared group identity that can be reasonably traced between the Native American human remains and associated funerary objects and the Citizen Potawatomi Nation, Oklahoma; Forest County Potawatomi Community, Wisconsin; Hannahville Indian Community, Michigan; Pokagon Band of Potawatomi Indians, Michigan and Indiana; and Prairie Band Potawatomi Nation (previously listed as the Prairie Band of Potawatomi Nation, Kansas)." Public notice was given, but as of this writing, no nation has claimed the remains.

"Dead Man's Curve" is a dangerous place to travel, and accidents still take place on this stretch of road. I had a relative crash in this location who I believed to be a pretty good driver. I asked him what happened, and he said he did not know; one minute he was on the road, and the next he was not. So whether you believe in accursed land or not, it is probably best to always drive defensively and obey the speed limit.

CHAPTER 8

THE WALKER TAVERNS

CAMBRIDGE TOWNSHIP

The Walker Taverns at one point in history were on one property. This is no longer the case, but because historically they are connected, I will share these reported hauntings in one entry. The first home was built at the crossroads of the Old Chicago and La Plaisance Bay Roads circa 1832. A migrant couple from New York, Sylvester and Lucy Walker, purchased the property from Calvin Snell and turned it into an inn, the Walker Tavern, in 1843. Sylvester had previously been a professional hatter. The Walkers ran a respectable and successful establishment. The Walker Tavern had a bar, dining room and overnight accommodations. Note that in this period, travelers shared communal beds. The Walkers had a small farm to supplement their larder. Lucy was renowned for her meals, especially her baking. The book *Michigan Off the Beaten Path* reported, "A typical supper at Walker Tavern might include stewed chicken, biscuits, cornbread, and applesauce cake or pumpkin pie." In 1847, Sylvester, a Democrat, served as the congressional representative for Lenawee County. He also served as a road commissioner.

Though the Walker Tavern had a good reputation, it should be noted that stagecoach stops varied in quality and safety. There were also additional perils on the road. Notoriously, highwaymen like Sile Doty roamed the region, posing a threat to travelers. The first ghost story connected to Walker Tavern is centered on such an unwary traveler. One version of the legend, recounted in an article by Leanne Smith, follows:

One night a traveler rode up on a black horse. He carried a great deal of money, which fact became known, possibly through his own garrulity. He was assigned the room now shown, but did not put his horse in the stable, instead, tying it to an oak tree in the woods behind the house. The following morning the traveler was found dead in his bed, stabbed with a dagger, and a large pool of blood had collected on the floor. The excited discoverers of the corpse left the room for a short time, and when they returned, the body was gone. The horse too had disappeared.

The version that I first heard was embellished more in that the man had been playing cards and drinking heavily in the tavern, thus letting unscrupulous people know of his wealth. The spirits of the murdered man and his trusty steed are rumored to still be searching for each other on the property. Some have claimed to have seen a phantom stallion wandering in the woods. Though certainly a cautionary tale, it has never been verified by primary source evidence. Later, entrepreneur Reverend Hewitt would stage a "murder room" in the tavern, including using red paint to re-create the pool of blood as a tourist draw.

The second area with a ghostly legend is the Brick Walker Tavern. Currently, it is a private event venue business and is not a part of the Cambridge Junction State Historic Park. The business thrived for the Walkers, so they decided to expand. Sylvester Walker had the new inn built in 1853, a fine three-story structure across the road from the wooden Walker

This postcard depicts both the original Walker Tavern and the Brick Walker Tavern at Cambridge Junction. Frederick Hewitt purchased the property to open an antique shop and tourist attraction. *Author's collection.*

This postcard features the notorious "murder room" at Walker Tavern, a popular Irish Hills attraction. This display was based on the story of a traveler who met an untimely end. *Author's collection.*

Tavern. The Brick Walker Tavern had a dining room and tavern on the first floor, guest rooms on the second floor and a ballroom on the third floor. Public events and dances were often held in the ballroom. It is from this fact that a story sprang of a party-turned-tragedy at the Brick Walker Tavern. According to the tale, a large dance was held on New Year's Eve, December 31, 1863. People were drinking and dancing and reveling the night away. Perhaps the party was more intense as a way to forget the war that continued to drag on. Though Michigan was far away from any battlefront, many still had absent loved ones serving to defend the Union. It began to snow, and at first, it added to the magical ambiance of the social gathering. It is lovely to watch the flakes floating outside while one is nice and toasty inside. But soon the snowfall began to get heavier and heavier.

Experienced Michiganders know to keep an eye on such storms and exit before the roads get too dangerous. Most left the ballroom for home. Unfortunately, at this gathering, some young people did not understand the gravity of the situation. Their desire to usher in the new year clouded their judgment. This would end up being a fatal mistake. Franklin Dewey recounted the tale: "As New Year's Eve drew on, some more venturesome boldly tried to reach their homes. All were badly frostbitten. A young man with his sister drove madly down the Monroe Turnpike [M-50]. He almost perished but reached home with his sister dead in the carriage beside him." Those who believe the Brick Walker Tavern to be haunted by this event note that sensitive people often feel overwhelming sadness and cold spots. Paranormal investigators think that such experiences may be physical manifestations of a spirit.

Several people indeed perished in Michigan alone in the Midwest Blizzard of 1864 with its driving snow, frigid temperatures and strong winds. The *Detroit Free Press* reported, "The thermometer indicated twenty degrees below zero, and the wind blew a gale for forty-eight hours from the southwest." I could find many articles about unfortunate people who froze to death in the blizzard. One of these accounts that affected me the most was the death of an entire family who was discovered by a stagecoach driver. The *Cass County Republican* related the dreadful scene:

> *The stage driver coming from Crown Point to Centerville, discovered the house in which the family lived burned down. As he passed on he found the father and two sons frozen to death. The boys were clasped in the ice-bound arms of their father. About a quarter of a mile further on the daughter was found with a shawl wrapped closely around her. A little further on were found the corpses of the mother and the two youngest children. The mother was standing erect, in a snow-drift, with the two children in her arms.*

Unfortunately, I could not find a primary source confirmation of the death of a young woman near the Brick Walker Tavern region similar to the tale related by Dewey. It would not surprise me if such an event happened, but I cannot verify it.

By 1864, as the stagecoach began to be replaced by the train, business dropped at Walker Tavern. Sylvester and Lucy decided to sell their property to a former stagecoach driver and mail carrier, Francis Dewey, originally from Canada. Dewey hoped it would continue to be a successful business and also used it as his family's home. Additionally, Dewey had a great interest in local history, serving for many years as the president of the Michigan Pioneer and Historical Society. The Dewey family sold the property to Reverend Frederick Hewitt and his wife, Edna, in 1921, and they began to deal in antiques. Reverend Hewitt retired in 1922 and developed both taverns as tourist attractions.

The Irish Hills region with its lakes and rolling hills had served as a vacation center in the county. With the growth of automobile tourism in the 1920s made possible with better roads, many places of interest were developed there. Some from that period were Irish Hills observation towers, water slides and the St. Joseph Shrine. At Walker Tavern, Hewitt's collection of curiosities included a trading post, a historic oak tree, antiques, relics and rooms dedicated to reputed visitors of the past, like James Fenimore

Cooper, Daniel Webster and Harriet Martineau. The Hewitt family also built a family home on the land.

The final area rumored to be haunted is the Hewitt House, which now serves as the visitors' center for Cambridge Junction Historic State Park. In 1929, Reverend Frederick Hewitt's son, James, built a Greek Revival–style home for his family on the Walker Tavern property. This architectural type was originally in fashion from 1825 to 1860, and the home featured a low-pitch roof, cornice lines with a wide divided band of trim, an entry porch supported by prominent columns, a narrow transom and sidelights providing decoration around the front door. I first began volunteering at the park around 2008 and served on the Friends of Walker Tavern board for a time. I primarily created and led educational programs. Some volunteers reported unease to me while working in the Hewitt House—like they were being watched by an unseen presence. Others reported hearing odd noises and footsteps when they knew they were the only ones in the center. Some speculated that perhaps the spirit was one of the members of the Hewitt family. Ghost hunter Jeff Westover, in his blog, reported his encounter at the house:

> *In October 2011, on the morning of a Victorian Halloween event at the Walker Tavern Park, I had an encounter with what I think was the spirit of a young child on the stairway of the Hewitt House (visitors' center). I was halfway up the staircase when I felt the cool breeze of something passing me extremely fast and saw a smallish blur ascending the steps. At the same time I felt the breeze, I clearly heard quick footsteps and a girl's voice say, "I'm having fun." The blurry apparition disappeared as soon as it reached the top of the stairway.*

In my approximately five years of service to the park, I was frightened only once. I was giving a tour to elementary schoolchildren, and we went into the barn on the property. As I began to point out features and hands-on activities for them to try, we all heard a rustling in one corner of the barn. The unexpected noise startled everyone. It turned out to be a family of raccoons that had temporarily nested in the barn. I quickly ushered the students out because it would ruin a field trip if one of them contracted rabies. I certainly was more frightened by that prospect than by any ghost. This area of Lenawee County could certainly be considered the most haunted due to the number of legends attached to the Walker Taverns, but I have many wonderful memories connected to this place. Whether ghost hunting or not, I strongly encourage a visit to Cambridge Junction.

CHAPTER 9

SIAM SCHOOL

CAMBRIDGE JUNCTION

The Northwest Ordinance of 1787 initially set up the educational system for the territory. In 1809, the Michigan Territory taxed families with children to support public education, and in 1827, the legislature passed a public school law. Historians Bruce A. Rubenstein and Lawrence E. Zwiewacz stated, "Every township with fifty or more residents had to hire a teacher of good morals to offer instruction, over a six-month period, in reading, writing, arithmetic, English, French, and decent behavior. If a township possessed over 200 inhabitants it was required to have a higher school which offered advanced training in the basic skills as well as Latin." Though not initially strongly enforced, this set the precedent that the state set the course of study, regular state inspections, and the length of the school year. The state assembly passed free public primary education in 1869 and compulsory attendance in 1871.

In 1825, Tecumseh had the first public schoolhouse constructed in the county. It was constructed of logs, as was typical of that period. Brick one-room schoolhouses became more commonplace after the Civil War. Notably, Lenawee County had one of the earliest integrated schools in the United States, the Woodstock Manual Labor Institute (incorporated in 1848), and the first reformatory school for females in the state, the Michigan Industrial Home for Girls (established in 1879). In 1856, a group of teachers formed the Lenawee County Teachers' Association for professional development. Early public schools were ungraded, but over time, more districts became graded. In the 1897 state superintendent report of students included in the school census, Michigan had 5,972 students in ungraded districts and 7,135 students in graded districts. Unfortunately, the quality of instruction often was substandard given the low pay, and it was not until 1925 that teachers were required to have a year of training.

In 1852, Isaac and Hannah Powers donated land for a district school in Cambridge Township. This first school in the Irish Hills district was constructed of logs and called the Siam School in honor of the Potawatomi leader Siam. A brick one-room schoolhouse would replace this structure in 1862. A short history of the school describes, "As one stands in the doorway of the school named for the famous chieftain and looks to the south across the little valley between the two lakes, a lovely wooded elevation meets the gaze." The two lakes are Allen and Wolf, near Dead Man's Curve, an earlier entry in this book. Similarly to the graves unearthed at Dead Man's Curve, a corpse was also found on the Powerses' property. When men were digging a hole for a cistern, the corpse of a child was found preserved, but when the air hit the body, it disintegrated. Not long after, a Potawatomi woman stopped by the Powerses' home requesting the body of her child. When told that the body was no more, she wailed in grief that the grave had been disturbed. This emotionality seemed strange to the Powerses, as the corpse must have been very ancient. Yet the Powerses failed to understand the sacred nature of burials and the importance of the ancestral relations.

Some of the first teachers at the Siam School were Jane Ayres, Alzina Blackmer and Mary Stafford. Women were often preferred as educators, as they could be paid less than their male counterparts. Teachers usually boarded with local families. A former Siam student, Beulah Ingraham, recalled, "I lived on Person Highway in the yellow house and the farm that was on the south side of Stony Lake and now has several new homes built where my dad used to farm the land and all. Walked to Siam School with Bernice and Stanley Blowers, Marie Knapp and it was great." It seems as if many shared her love for the school, as for decades there were regular reunions. In 1931, over three hundred former Siam scholars returned for a ceremony to dedicate a marker and boulder noting the school's significance.

Due to the importance of free agricultural labor that children provided, the school term started in the fall and ran until early spring. The nine-month academic year did not come to pass until 1905. The average class size in these one-room schoolhouses was thirty students, ages four to eighteen. Memorization and recitation were common teaching techniques, focusing on reading, writing, arithmetic and geography. Punishments for misbehavior were swift because maintaining control of the classroom was viewed as

This interior view of the Wooden Old Stone School in Lenawee County, near Onsted, shows an example of what the Siam Schoolhouse of Cambridge Junction may have looked like before renovation. *Author photo.*

paramount. Corporal punishments such as having one's knuckles hit with a ruler or one's backside with a rod were commonplace. Additionally, discipline that ridiculed the wayward student was utilized, such as wearing a dunce cap and sitting in the corner or standing on one leg in front of the class for an hour.

By the 1870s, in order to better utilize resources, many communities began to consolidate and form union schools and close the one-room schoolhouses. By 1873, Lenawee County had 189 district schools. In the twentieth century, a push began in the state to consolidate these schools. In the more rural areas, one-room schoolhouses survived into the 1920s, and some like the Siam School lasted even later. Siam School closed in 1949.

The Siam School would go on to serve other purposes. At some point, an extension was added to the school, and it housed a few businesses over the years, such as an antique store and a bakery. People have also lived in it as a home. As of this writing, it is a private residence. There have been reports by residents in the past of unusual activities in the former school. The homeowner would find pictures taken off the walls and lying facedown on the floor. Books likewise would be found out of place and sometimes fly off the shelves. Those books were romance stories that perhaps offended the ghost's sensibilities. If I were a ghost, I would throw romance novels, not because I am prudish, but because I think they set up unrealistic and harmful relationship models. I would also hurl the works of Ayn Rand and Diane Ravitch, for similar reasons. According to paranormal investigator Jeff Westover, the owner of the former Siam School asked a local medium to contact the spirit in hopes of releasing it from the property. This sensitive claimed that the spirit was Jane Ayres, the first schoolmistress. There are no reports on whether the specter of this former teacher was released from the property by the psychic or not. Given that some of the best and worst experiences are forged during our primary and secondary school years, I can imagine that the Siam School is still haunting the memories of some former students.

CHAPTER 10
THE CLINTON INN

CLINTON

The Clinton Inn, I can state with authority, is haunted. Every October for approximately the past five years, the inn has been decorated as a Halloween attraction, the Haunted Hotel. Each year has a different theme. Some examples over the years include a scary asylum, a postapocalyptic world and a spooky hotel, of course. This October event is extremely popular and typically sells out weeks in advance. The rest of the year, this business primarily serves as a wedding and event center. I personally think this would be the perfect location for a Halloween wedding.

The Clinton Inn was built on the location of the first log home of Alpheus Kies, the founder of Clinton. Kies was born in Woodstock, Connecticut, in 1788, and then lived in New York for several years with his wife, Elizabeth, before they moved to Michigan in 1829. Of Alpheus, the *Memoirs of Lenawee County, Michigan* reported, "He secured from the government 240 acres of land, that is now Clinton township, and both the village and the township were named by him, in honor of DeWitt Clinton, one of the early governors of the state of New York….Alpheus Kies was a man of strong mentality, marked individuality, and much initiative power so that he naturally became a leader in the pioneer community." As the Kies home was the only one for approximately forty miles, often it served as an inn as well. The structure was often referred to as the Clintonian during this period. When the modern Clinton Inn opened on Thanksgiving Day 1901, it was originally called the Clintonian Hotel, in remembrance of the original log structure on the site. Alonzo Clark was the proprietor of the impressive three-story brick structure with thirty-five rooms. For much of its history, the Clinton Inn has served as

This lovely structure has served countless people in its many incarnations as a hotel, restaurant, apartment complex, coffee shop and event venue. *Author photo.*

a lodging place as its primary business. A variety of renovations have also taken place over the decades. The current owners, the Huffaker family—father Marvin, with his children Austin and Jasmine—give a nice overview on the Clinton Inn website:

> *Running water and plumbing were added during the early 1900s. Many of the existing hotel rooms were converted into bathrooms, which cut the number of rooms down significantly. At some point, a steam boiler heating system was installed (still in use to this day). During the 1960's–1970's, the entire building was converted into apartments. Then during the 1980's, the 2nd floor was converted back to hotel rooms while the 3rd story*

> *apartments remained. Also, during the mid 1980s, the adjacent two-story building (formerly a retail store) was purchased, joined to the hotel, and the retail space was converted into a dining room. A ballroom was added above the dining room and connected to the 2nd floor via a hallway just past the main staircase. In 2023 the larger dining room was converted into a ballroom and used to host weddings and other events. The original smaller dining room has been converted into a banquet room and is used to host smaller parties and events.*

I first fell in love with the Clinton Inn in the 1990s, when it still offered lodging but was perhaps better known as a restaurant. My fiancé wanted to take me to a nice restaurant, so he chose this one. After we married, we regularly had a date night at this inn that had delicious food and wonderful ambiance. When ownership changed in 2019, this turned out to not be the best timing to continue a restaurant, especially with the COVID-19 outbreak. I have so many cherished memories of amazing meals at the restaurant with loved ones, and I miss it very much, so in that way the Clinton Inn haunts me personally. There are also, however, reports of strange phenomena at the inn.

Guests and employees have seemingly experienced doors opening and closing without the aid of any person. Orbs have been captured by photograph. Footsteps have been heard in an upstairs portion when it was empty. Vacated and cleaned guest rooms have been checked, only to find something in disarray, like pictures off the wall. In a Facebook post from September 25, 2019, an administrator of the site posted the following account:

> *Late last night after things had quieted down for the evening and we were all closed up. Nobody else was in the building. Jasmine and I were on the main level working at a new desk we had just bought for the lobby. We were setting up a computer to help deal with reservations and such. Austin was upstairs on the 2nd floor taking a shower. He texted us and asked if someone was knocking on his door and what did we want. Let's just say that it wasn't us, and Austin freaked out a little.*

As if those types of experiences are not creepy enough, there is a story of the place being visited by a woman in white. At times, she is said to wander the halls of the inn. There is no background on why she inhabits this place or her name. However, there is a long-standing motif of such a ghost, sometimes called a White Lady, in several traditions globally. Brian Haughton notes in his analysis in the work *Famous Ghost Stories: Legends and*

The original Clinton Inn was a stagecoach stop on U.S. 12. After it fell into disrepair, Henry Ford moved the building to Greenfield Village in Dearborn to restore it. *Library of Congress.*

Lore, "The tradition of a ghostly woman in white, a class of ghost so called because of the white color of her dress, is found in a number of different countries....This particular ghostly motif can have a number of different functions, depending on the context and culture in which it is recorded." Often these earthbound female spirits are believed to have been victims of romantic betrayals that resulted in either their murder or suicide.

One would be remiss not to mention the first Clinton Inn. This stagecoach stop, constructed in 1831, was one of many such establishments on the route between Detroit and Chicago, modern-day U.S. 12. It changed hands several times throughout its history. By the 1920s, the inn was in a very poor condition. In 1927, Henry Ford bought the crumbling building for his historical attraction located in Dearborn, Greenfield Village. After extensive historic preservation, the renamed Eagle Tavern opened for people to tour in 1929. One of the wonderful aspects of this place is that, since 1982, it has operated as an actual restaurant and served a menu based on fare and refreshments that would have been available in the 1850s. The book *Michigan Haunts: Public Places, Eerie Spaces* shared, "There have been sightings of a man and a woman hanging out in the bar area, dressed in 19th century clothes. People think that they are costumed guides at the Village, yet when approached, the 'barflies' disappear, sometimes right into the walls." I completely understand the desire to spend time in one's favorite restaurant even throughout all eternity. Perhaps I will join the Lady in White at the Clinton Inn after I pass away.

CHAPTER 11

WILLIAM G. THOMPSON HOUSE MUSEUM

HUDSON

Unlike most of the haunted houses included in this book, the William G. Thompson House can be toured inside and out, as it was turned into a public museum in 2004. Some of the special highlights of its collection include Asian art, Victorian furniture and a formal garden. The gorgeous 1890 Queen Anne–style house served as the abode for three generations of the Thompson family in Hudson. This Victorian housing design was at its height of popularity between 1880 and 1910, typified by patterned shingles, an asymmetrical façade, a porch that extends along one or both sidewalls, cutaway bay windows and a steeply pitched roof with a prominent front-facing gable. The Thompson House also exhibits beautiful spindlework, which is a principal subtype of this architectural form.

The first owner of this beautiful home, Gamaliel Ingham "G.I." Thompson, was born in 1843 just outside the Adirondacks in Fort Ann, New York. In 1861, at the age of eighteen, he immigrated to Hudson, along with his brothers, for better opportunities. They had family who lived in the town who could make the transition easier. G.I. worked as a clerk and bookkeeper for a general store and grain dealer, eventually becoming a partner in the business. His economic rise was interrupted by the Civil War, but afterward, he returned home and went into banking. He worked for Perkins, Osborn & Company, becoming a partner. In 1867, he formed the private Thompson Brothers Banking Company with his brothers William and Royal. On October 22, 1892, they reorganized the Thompson Saving Bank as a public bank, with William as president,

Gamaliel as vice president and Royal on the board of directors. G.I. married local woman Sophia Williams in 1879. Later, their son, William, would take over the bank, followed by his son, William. Each generation, in turn, would live in the home at 101 Summit Street.

When one visits this museum, one is struck by the extent of the collection. The last William to live in the home, a confirmed bachelor, loved antiques and the hunt to add to his displays. Particularly noteworthy are his jade figurines, but the whole museum is a feast for the eyes. Victorian furniture from his grandparents G.I. and Sophia is on prominent display in this house museum, as well as the most Oriental rugs I have ever seen in one home. Several photos of his parents, William and Louise, decorate the place, giving it a cozy atmosphere. It was explained to me on my visit that the family archive was quite extensive, containing photographs, receipts and letters. The Thompsons stressed to all family members the importance of taking care of relatives and the community. Donations were made to local organizations such as the United Methodist Church, Hudson Museum, Hudson Library and city parks. The large carriage house on the property serves as the visitors' center and has additional family items on display.

The museum holds several events during the year in the home, such as genealogy classes, antique appraisal events, a Christmas luncheon and Tea on the Porch. In October, ghost hunt tours are offered that quickly sell out. The phenomena that draw paranormal investigators to the home include reports of lights flickering, curtains moving, unusual noises and figures spotted in the windows. The root of some of this may lie in the fact that the last owner was a notorious night owl and often worked late rearranging his collections. Even now as a museum, the work of running and maintaining such an operation takes place often outside regular hours.

On the other hand, there were family members who passed away in the home—for example, G.I. Thompson at age eighty-three in 1926, Louise Thompson at age seventy-two in 1962 and William G. Thompson at age ninety-one in 2004. The Ohio Researchers of Banded Spirits (ORBS) has led investigations at the home. Founded in 2007 in Fremont, this group has examined hundreds of sites and been featured on television programs such as Animal Planet's *The Haunted*, Biography Channel's *My Ghost Story* and The History Channel's *Haunted History*. ORBS co-founder Chris Page once explained in a *News-Messenger* interview, "We're mostly scientific-based because it's easier to prove something on video and something on audio." The organization also does historical research before an inspection and at times includes a medium who attempts to contact spirits. During a

The William G. Thompson House Museum in Hudson holds many yearly events. One of its most popular is a ghost hunt led by professional paranormal investigators. *Author photo.*

recent examination of the William G. Thompson House, one of the ORBS investigators commented that they felt the presence of a little boy.

In 1942, a young boy tragically died on the property. The Foster family lived two doors down from the Thompson house. Hal and Julia Foster, along with their two children, James and Margery, had moved to Hudson from Neosho, Missouri, in 1940. Hal came to Michigan to serve as the ice cream department manager for the PET Milk Company. According to oral tradition, the neighborhood children would regularly visit the Thompsons' garden to look at their koi pond. At suppertime, the understanding was for the children to go back to their own homes. One late afternoon, three-year-old James, instead of going home, hid so he could return to look at the fish some more. He fell into the pond and drowned. On August 14, 1942, the *Daily Telegram* reported, "The child had been playing out of doors and when Mrs. Foster did not see him in the yard she began a search and found the body floating on the surface of the water. He had been out of sight for only a few minutes. No one saw him fall into the water." Firefighters worked for an hour attempting to revive him. After this devastating loss, the Foster family moved back to Missouri. The koi pond no longer exists, as soon after, in grief, William Thompson the elder destroyed it.

What I find particularly commendable about the William G. Thompson House Museum is its dedication to not only preserving this historic structure and the Thompson family history but also to providing educational and entertaining opportunities for the community. In my experience with museum studies, often museum organizations avoid any exploration of ghostly legends that are attached to the property for fear of this impacting its reputation. I find it refreshing when nonprofits are open to a variety of programming opportunities to serve the public, whether that includes a scavenger hunt, an Easter egg hunt or a ghost hunt.

CHAPTER 12
TREADWELL HOUSE
HUDSON

Coincidentally, a second reputedly haunted location in Hudson was also built by a banker. However, while the Thompson family legacy was one of honesty and community service, William Treadwell fell on the other end of the spectrum. His misdeeds severely damaged the town. Additionally, unlike the Thompsons, who inhabited their beautiful home for generations, Treadwell never had the opportunity to live in his Italian villa mansion due to his murder. His story might be a good illustration of the adage that crime never pays.

William Treadwell was a local, having grown up in the Hudson area on a farm. After graduation from Hudson schools, Treadwell completed a business course at Oberlin College in Ohio. Rumor had it that he did not complete his studies there due to a romantic entanglement with a young woman from whom he needed to escape. Upon returning to Hudson, he worked for a time as a clerk and then got a job at the People's State Bank. Treadwell rose quickly through the organization with a reputation for punctuality and trustworthiness. He became a partner and then, with investment from his father, Urias, became a co-owner of the bank in 1859, though Urias would in effect be a silent partner. *The Bean Creek Valley* history recounted of William Treadwell, "He had by his pleasant ways and obliging disposition made himself very popular among the farmers and businessmen, and his safe contained large sums of money deposited on account of such friendship." In 1862, William married a woman from Huron County, Ohio, Mary E. Hester, daughter of Samuel and Emily. She had also grown up in a farming family. Not long after William and Mary wed, construction began on their home north of downtown Hudson on Highway U.S. 127.

Its location coincided with what had been suggested by the famous Philadelphian architect Samuel Sloan as the best site for this style, a few miles outside a city on a hill by a highway. Sloan also noted that this type of house speaks of the inhabitant as a "man of wealth who wishes in a quiet way to enjoy his wealth. It speaks of him as a person of educated and refined tastes who can appreciate the beautiful both in art and nature; who accustomed to all the ease and luxury of a city life, is now enjoying the more pure and elevating pleasures of the county." The Italian villa style, favored between 1842 and 1880, had many similarities with the Italianate style. There were two major digressions in that the villa had an irregular layout and an impressive tower. Treadwell's mansion was a two-story brick structure constructed on a slight hill overlooking the road. It is truly puzzling why Treadwell made certain decisions that he knew would mean he would never live in this beautiful and fashionable home.

The banker William Treadwell never inhabited the beautiful Hudson mansion that was built for him. Instead, his crimes ultimately led to his premature death. *National Register of Historic Places.*

It is uncertain when Treadwell first hatched the plan to steal from his bank. In early January 1864, he requested and received several loans from other midwestern banks. Along with those funds, he completely cleaned out the safe from his bank of approximately $60,000 and absconded on January 20. Treadwell met up with his wife and father-in-law in Ohio, who knew of the plot, though the authorities did not realize this at the time. Unfortunately for the trio, the law caught up with them in Mansfield on February 11. Treadwell was arrested and taken back to Adrian, Michigan, to stand trial. His father, Urias, though having nothing to do with his son's crime, became a community outcast. He sold his property and moved to Iowa.

On July 1, a jury convicted Treadwell. When his wife, Mary, embraced him before he was taken away by the bailiff, she slipped Treadwell $800 to assist him in his plan to escape. While in jail, Treadwell formed a quick partnership with convicted horse thief John Cowell. Flashing his wad of cash and telling Cowell that he could have a share of the stolen money now being safeguarded by his father-in-law, Treadwell convinced Cowell to help him escape. They broke out that same afternoon. At some point, Cowell grew tired of his traveling companion and decided to rob and kill Treadwell rather than trust in the promised greater gains. Treadwell was beaten and shot by Cowell on July 4, and his badly decomposed remains were not discovered until almost two weeks later in some woods outside Napoleon, Ohio. His dentist had to identify him using dental records. Of Treadwell's murder, the *Bryan Democrat* editorialized, "A heartless and unfeeling wretch, he richly deserved the dog's death that he died, and for him the only regret is that Cowell was not his authorized executioner."

Authorities tracked Cowell to Cleveland, Ohio. He was arrested and returned to Napoleon, where he was tried and convicted of first-degree murder. Executed by hanging on July 7, 1865, Cowell confessed to his crime. Neither Mary Treadwell nor her father, Samuel Hester, was charged as accessories to the embezzlement. There was strong evidence that Hester hid the money for Treadwell, and in 1868, a civil lawsuit ordered a judgment of $38,514.99 against Hester. These damages were to be paid to some of Treadwell's creditors, though legal fees impacted the true award. Mary remarried in 1866 to Dr. J.S. Stough, a man approximately seventeen years her senior, and they moved to Waterloo, Indiana. Dr. Stough would outlive Mary, as she died four years after their wedding. Likely her death at age twenty-five was connected to childbirth complications, as her tombstone also notes the death of an infant daughter.

The apparitions seen in the Treadwell house are of a mother and infant. A former owner of the home had two separate incidents while she lived there. In the first encounter, a visiting relative sleeping in a spare bedroom awoke to see a woman rocking a baby in the room's rocking chair. The pair then faded away. The guest recounted the story, but the owner kept this to herself, as she did not want anyone to think that her relative was of unsound mind. Years passed without incident until another friend spent the night in the spare room. That guest woke up and saw a woman and child standing near the rocking chair before disappearing in front of the astonished guest. As the owner had never shared the first incident with anyone, this encounter was taken more seriously. In researching the history of the house, I have uncovered no deaths in the home. So could this be a haunted rocking chair? There have been previous accounts of cursed furniture, such as the chairs of Belcourt Castle in Newport, Rhode Island, or a bedroom set sold by a Rowan County, North Carolina Habitat for Humanity ReStore. Or could one haunt a home that was meant to be theirs but that one never got a chance to live in, like Mary Treadwell? If so, then could a soul inhabit a place that was never theirs but that they strongly admired? If that were the case, the options for a ghostly house hunt would be something to look forward to in the afterlife for many spirits.

CHAPTER 13

DEVILS LAKE

MANITOU BEACH

Devils Lake is a beautiful 1,330-acre lake, the largest in the county, and I have fished in it several times. This body of water has several folktales connected to it. The commonality between the tales is that all attempt to describe how the body of water earned the moniker "Devils Lake." There are a few variations on the most widely shared story currently—the romance of a pair of star-crossed lovers. The daughter of the Potawatomi Chief Oroneka, Izone, fell in love with Indimane, a man her father considered to be an unsuitable marital choice. Furthermore, the chief had decided for his daughter to marry a member of another tribe, the Wyandotte, in order to create an alliance. Izone and Indimane decide to elope so that they would always be together. The plan was to leave in the middle of the night, cross the lake to a set of horses on the other side and make their escape. For an unknown reason, an evil spirit of the lake overturned their canoe, thwarting their objective.

The next morning, the body of Indimane washed up on the shore. Chief Oroneka sat vigil in a stone chair on the northeast shore, later to be called the Devil's Chair, scanning the body of water in vain for his daughter. Her body was never recovered, and it is claimed that her corpse still rests at the deepest part of the lake, called the Devil's Hole. A village to the south of the lake would be called Manitou Beach. In Vogel's study of Native American place names in Michigan, he explained:

> *The Algonquian tribes of this region called all spirits, good or bad, manitou. The great or good spirit was kitchi-manitou, a bad spirit was*

> *matchi-manitou, and ordinary spirits were simply manitou. Countrywide, it is not uncommon to find the name Manitou in association with the "Devil" in place-names, for many whites, all Indian deities were devils. The United States Geological Survey lists twenty-two Michigan place-names containing the word Devil or Devils, and it appears likely that most of them represent a white translation of Manitou.*

For several generations, the Devil's Chair rock formation was a sightseeing destination. Postcards were even made of the stone. Unfortunately, with greater economic development by the late 1920s, the unusually shaped boulder is thought to have been broken into pieces and carted away. Similarly, a large mound once called the Devil's Wigwam, near the outlet of the lake, is no more. The location called the Devil's Hole is sixty-three feet deep, and no fish or live vegetation exist at this cold-water spring. It is very apparent that this folktale, like many myths, attempted to explain a natural phenomenon to a pre-scientific audience.

It should be noted that there are other variants of the legend. In another version, there was no love story. In this tale, Potawatomi Chief Mitteau (also spelled Meteau and Metataugh) had a daughter who, though a very strong swimmer, drowned in the lake, and her body was never recovered. The only explanation that made sense to the grief-stricken chief was that evil spirits had seized her. An early settler to the area, Frances Dewey, knew Chief Mitteau personally and recollected, "When I first knew him his age was about fifty; strong and vigorous in personal appearance; tall, well-formed, with a clear, sharp, black eye, and a general bearing that reminded one of a prince of the forest. It is recorded that 'fire-water' was the cause of this brave chief's death."

There are legends that give a different account of the chief's death that were most widely circulated in the 1950s. In one, his daughter was kidnapped by a man—in some narratives a Mohawk and in others a Wyandotte—and the chief pursued them in a canoe. A whirlpool created by evil spirits swallowed his boat at the location of the Devil's Hole. In another telling, it was Chief Mitteau's beloved who was stolen by a Mohawk man, with the same sad ending. The death of Chief Mitteau by whirlpool inspired the dedication on October 1, 1954, of a marker to him by the Lenawee County Historical Society at the Devils Lake public boat launching site. It reads, "In memory of Chief Meteau of the Pottawattomie Tribe through whose tragic death Devils Lake received its name. The tribe inhabited the territory until they were driven out in 1834."

A lesser-known story of Devils Lake appeared in a 1903 edition of *Forest and Stream*. In this telling, this place gets its negative name due to an event in which two people lost their lives. This misfortune reportedly took place around 1740, when two Native American women attempted to cross the lake when the ice was too thin and subsequently drowned.

As is common to most legends, little can be verified in any of these stories. Here is what can be substantiated about the historical origins of Devils Lake and its nearby village, Manitou Beach. There was a Potawatomi village located at Devils Lake through the early 1830s, and Chief Mitteau did live in the area. White settlement began circa 1833. The Potawatomi and other Indigenous groups were forced from their lands through a series of treaties. The Potawatomi relinquished title to their last properties in the Treaty of Chicago of 1833 and acquiesced to move to reservations west of the Mississippi. At this time, an estimated 6,000 to 7,000 people of this nation lived in Michigan. Approximately 1,200 Potawatomi were removed to Kansas, and perhaps as many as 2,500 fled to Canada. Historians Dunbar and May noted the resilience of the community:

> *A considerable number of Potawatomi, however, remained in Michigan. Some eluded the government agents. Others escaped during the trip westward and returned to Michigan. In some of the treaties, grants of land were made to individual Indians, and although the recipients in many instances sold their land to white settlers, there probably were a considerable number who retained their land....In addition, some Potawatomi who lived in Wisconsin in the 1830s moved up into the Upper Peninsula where their descendants live on the Hannahville Reservation in Menominee County.*

I have not so far found the names Oroneka, Izone or Indimane in the historical record, and there are irregularities in two of the names that do not conform with Potawatomi language structure. This most popular story also does not reflect Potawatomi culture in two important ways. First, though parents helped in the selection of marriage partners, the person to be wed, male or female, had final say. Izone would not have been forced to marry someone. Second, the reason for the arranged marriage of a political alliance was much more common in European culture. The Milwaukee Public Museum page describes further about Potawatomi culture:

> *The clans were exogamous, so individuals could not marry a person of the same clan. Upon marriage, a couple usually went to live with the husband's*

family, so each summer village included a group of men and their children who were members of the same clan and members of other clans who had married members of the main clan in that village. The intermarriages of the clans created links between different villages, and these links were both reinforced and encouraged by trade and other bonds. These bonds existed not only within the Potawatomi tribe but also with nearby villages of related Ottawa and Ojibwe, whose members freely intermarried or lived with the Potawatomi.

As to whether someone drowned in the pre-contact past, it is not beyond the realm of possibility that some tragedy on the lake led to its name of Devils Lake; it just cannot be confirmed by primary sources.

Other tragedies have occurred in the more recent past that have caused some to claim the area still has evil spirits. As can be expected, there have been other people who have drowned in Devils Lake. Small planes have crashed into this body of water on two separate occasions with lives lost. During the Palm Sunday tornado outbreak of 1965, twelve tornados touched down in Michigan alone. Two F-4 tornados went through Lenawee County. At Manitou Beach, two churches, a dance pavilion and several

This postcard of Devils Lake shows a couple enjoying their canoe trip. However, several legends of this lake do not end so happily. *Author's collection.*

cottages were destroyed by the high winds, and eleven people lost their lives. The community came together and rebuilt the village. Similarly, when the restaurant the Manitou Beach Inn burned to the ground in 2010, it was reconstructed and reopened eighteen months later as the Manitou Bar and Grill. I think the survival of this community over the generations reflects its spirit as a place of resilience. Not a place of *kitchi-manitou* or *matchi-manitou* but simply *manitou.* The stories connected to this place also show how legends can grow and change over time.

CHAPTER 14
REX THEATRE
MORENCI

Perhaps the smell of hot, buttered popcorn creates nostalgia around movie theaters for me. Some of my happiest memories are of going to the movies with friends and family. From going to see *Pete's Dragon* (1977) with my father and sister, to sneaking in snacks while watching *Pretty in Pink* (1986), to taking a date to see *The Rocky Horror Picture Show* (1975) to see if he was cool enough to be my boyfriend (he was and we have been married for over thirty years now), films have been touchstones for key turning points in my life. With the advent of streaming, I do not go out to a physical theater as often, but when I do, I still get a rush of expectation and joy. I can imagine wanting to haunt such a place for all eternity.

One movie theater that has a reputation for being haunted in Lenawee County is the Rex Theatre. This 220-seat venue originally opened downtown as the Gem in 1916. It was a transitional venue in that it both booked vaudeville acts and showed short films. The proprietor was Martin Gay, and he ran the theater until 1921, when he moved on to other business pursuits, like collections and insurance. By this period, these types of movie houses were showing feature-length silent films by the major studios, such as Paramount, United Artists and Universal. The popular genres were romantic comedies, horror and action adventure. This theater continued to entertain audiences for generations.

Unfortunately, the Rex later closed and sat vacant for many years. In 2020, Tim Newsom, a Morenci resident, purchased and renovated the property. The *Daily Telegram* interviewed Newsom, who explained, "I have

The Rex Theatre has served as an entertainment venue for over one hundred years in Morenci. To see a movie at this one-screen theater is to step back in time. *Author photo.*

always liked this building and I used to go here regularly as a kid. It's been sitting there empty for at least 10 years and I'm a hands-on type of guy. I like projects and I like to keep myself busy. I acquired the theater because it seemed like a project that would be pretty fun. And I'm able to bring some history back to the city of Morenci." When Newsom bought the building, it was in very poor condition, with a leaking roof, crumpled marquee, broken windows, collapsing ceiling and parts of the brick structure crumbling. But with much hard work, the theater reopened for business on December 11, 2021. The Rex shows second-run films at a discounted rate and hosts special events like comedy shows.

Those who think that the Rex might be haunted describe feeling an uncomfortable, strange atmosphere in the theater. There have also been reports of full-bodied apparitions. In one instance posted to the Ghosts of America website, a customer was the only one watching a movie in the screening room. After the film was over, the person was leaving when they heard something behind them. They turned around and saw a small figure walking down the aisle. When the patron took a double take, the form had disappeared from the theater. In another elaborate tale on the same website, a patron stepped into the theater to see what film would be playing next. Initially, they did not find any employees around, so they started to leave when they heard someone call out, "How did you enjoy the film?" They then spotted an older gentleman wearing a maroon uniform, white gloves and a circular hat standing behind a counter. Confused, the customer left the theater and then recalled that the employees of the Rex wear regular street clothes.

No tragedy has yet been uncovered in the history of the Rex that might account for any haunting. Quite the opposite, as there are several positive news stories about this civic-minded theater. For example, in 1944, the Rex donated $224.34 to the Morenci Club for its March of Dimes fundraiser. It is wonderful that this historic movie theater persists and continues to foster a community spirit. Who is to say for certain if other types of spirits are not also sheltered by the Rex? Film as an artform certainly provides a form of immortality to its artists. When I see my favorite actors on the big screen like Ginger Rogers, James Dean, Clark Gable and Katharine Hepburn, they are very alive to me, even though they have been dead for generations.

CHAPTER 15
THE RIDGEWAY MONSTER
RIDGEWAY TOWNSHIP

Fantastical beasts existed cross-culturally in the mythologies of ancient cultures. A few of these creatures were frightening, like the Kraken, which sometimes dragged sailors to their watery doom. Some of these creatures were helpful, like the unicorn, whose horn had healing powers. Legends at times also imparted symbolic meanings to these critters. It should be noted that some of these mythological beings were found to actually exist, such as the gorilla, discovered in 1847, or the giant squid in 1852, which inspired the Kraken tales.

Even today, all across this great country of ours exist legends of animals without proof of existence, otherwise known as cryptids. Perhaps the most popular cryptid nationwide is Bigfoot. What is fascinating to me is that every state has its own mythical creatures, as well. For example, West Virginia has Mothman, Maryland has Chessie, New Jersey has the Jersey Devil and so on. In many instances, these beings are celebrated as a source of state pride, with festivals, art, music, clothing and other merchandise dedicated to their beast or beasts. The most well-known cryptid in our state is the Michigan Dogman.

As might be expected from its name, it is a frightening seven-foot-tall humanoid creature with a dog's head. The first account dates back to at least 1887 in Wexford County, Michigan, where a group of lumberjacks encountered the beast deep in the forest. The *Detroit Free Press* in its exploration of the longevity of this legend stated, "More modern accounts include that by a vanload of hippies who said they were harassed by the

This abandoned library, originally built in 1887 in Ridgeway, was named for Jonathan Hall (1801–1882). Hall migrated from Lyme, Connecticut, to become one of the first settlers in the area. *Author photo.*

Dogman near Cross Village in 1967. Police took an incident report in 1987 from people who said they saw such a creature in Luther. There are photos of something from the U.P.'s Garden Peninsula and Onaway in 2004 and unexplained tracks in the Waterloo Recreation Area in Chelsea in the late 1980s." There was also an 8mm film shot in the 1970s, similar in style to the 1967 Patterson-Grimlin footage of Bigfoot, which seemingly captured the Dogman. Unfortunately for cryptozoologists, it was a very good fake created by Mike Agrusa in 2007. There have been reported sightings of Dogman across the state, including Lenawee County. Michigan has other cryptids in various regions of the state, such as Pressie (a lake creature near Presque Isle) and Le Nain Rouge (the vengeful dwarf of Detroit), but most important for this book is the story of the Ridgeway Monster.

Ridgeway is a very tiny unincorporated community in a township of the same name located to the east of Tecumseh. It was officially founded in 1841 as a village, though settlement existed prior to that date. There were several successful farms and stockraising operations in the community. At one point, Ridgeway had its own post office, general store, school and public library. Today, very little remains of the village. There are a few homes, but there are also many historic abandoned buildings, such as the Jonathan Hall Memorial Library and the 1903 home two doors down from the library, to say nothing of several old dilapidated farms outside the former village. These desolate structures perhaps helped foster a modern legend of a cryptid lurking around the area. The first report of this creature dates to 1986.

A news article from around Halloween in the *Tecumseh Herald* reported that an unnamed realtor claimed some people in the community had seen a creature with red fur and green eyes that was acting like a peeping tom and looking into local homes' windows. This same realtor also stated that another home in Ridgeway had a poltergeist. Given the timing and vagueness of this account, one might be a bit suspicious, but the newspaper stated, "Interestingly enough, a comparable tale was also reported from a Tecumseh resident who was passing through Ridgeway and saw the same *monster*." I enjoy that the Ridgeway Monster is a bit atypical from most other cryptids in that instead of hiding from humans, it seemingly has a curiosity as to what we do in our homes.

Unfortunately, sightings did not continue to be reported in the township. Perhaps it was all just a hoax or filler added to the annual Halloween stories that populate local newspapers. But what if the monster just became better at hiding, like Bigfoot? It could easily squat in one of the empty properties, and maybe that is why it was looking into windows—to see which homes were inhabited. It could be that I would just enjoy a Ridgeway Monster festival in Lenawee County. I know that I would love to sport a T-shirt with our legendary creature. Truth be told, there is as much proof for the existence of this cryptid as there is for many other mysterious beasts. And keep in mind that scientists estimate that only 80 percent of the world's species have been discovered, so there is still a chance.

CHAPTER 16
THE SILVERS HOUSE
TECUMSEH

In the city of Tecumseh, there once was a home considered to be haunted. Though located in a nice neighborhood just a few blocks from the vibrant business district, it sat vacant for years. The handsome property was for sale, but no one made an offer due to its fearsome reputation. To someone unaware of its history, the two-story wooden framed house did not seem like a stereotypical haunted house, such as an abandoned and run-down mansion. Instead of being based on appearances, the Silvers family's home gained its notoriety due to the murder-suicide that took place there.

Frank L. Silvers had moved with his wife, Josephine, and daughters Edith and Ada to Tecumseh from nearby Clinton by 1882. Frank's father, John, according to the *Portrait and Biographical Album: Lenawee County*, was one of the founders of Clinton, and the family was very well respected, politically connected and wealthy. This *Album* further described:

> *In 1836 he was elected supervisor of Tecumseh township, which then comprised all of the present town of Clinton. He was again elected in 1838 and re-elected in 1839–1840. In 1847 he was again elected to the same office. He also served seven years as a tax collector and treasurer of the township. He was twice elected justice of the peace and served eight years. He has always been an active man and a thrifty farmer and has taken a great interest in the growth and development of the county. He says his farm has been a good one and has produced everything except a mortgage; that, it steadily refuses to do.*

Reportedly, Frank and Josephine relocated to the more urbane Tecumseh for better educational and cultural opportunities for Edith and Ada. Frank was a horse breeder and owner of the L Stables in town. He also managed an eighty-acre farm in Raisin Township. The *Detroit Free Press* on February 18, 1889, described Frank: "He was well-known throughout the surrounding county as a dealer in blooded horses, and the owner of the two stallions, Baron Rothschild and Bulletin. These were the chief source of his revenue and he was looked upon as a man in very comfortable circumstances. He was a man of abstemious habits, and well thought of by the community." The Silvers family was believed to be loving, prosperous and happy by those who knew them.

This impression shattered on the morning of Sunday, February 17, 1889. Neighbors thought it odd that no one was stirring at the Silvers household by 10:00 a.m., though they usually arose early. The curtains were drawn, and the home was too quiet. Neighbor and Town Marshal Thomas Kyle, with his wife, went to the house and attempted to rouse someone, but with no response. They broke in through the kitchen door to investigate and discovered that Frank Silvers had murdered his entire family using a revolver. He had shot himself in the head as well and was still clinging to life when the Kyles found him; he would die soon after on Monday morning. Frank was forty, Josephine was thirty-nine, Edith was eleven and Ada had just turned ten. Ada was murdered by her father the day after her birthday. A note dated February 16 from Frank was found at the scene addressed to Thomas Kyle and Lester Tribon. It read, in part:

> *Myself and family are going to take a trip, and we wish your assistance in disposing of our earthly accumulations. Through industry and economy, we have bunched a small pittance....Sell everything except my household furniture and my wife's and children's effects, namely clothes, jewelry, watches, etc., which give to her father....We don't want any funeral, just a few remarks by the Rev. Mr. Getchell, Universalist minister. Boys, there will be a great many questions asked in regard to us. Tell them they know as much as you about it. You know as well as anyone, and the whole thing is a mystery that solves the problem for us all.*

In addition to writing his last wishes on that Saturday, it later came to light in an inquest that Frank had purchased the murder weapon with bullets that morning at the store of Whiteneck, Bordine & Co., claiming he was going to use the revolver to kill rats. Later that evening, he attempted to

A final request of Frank Silvers was for an impressive tombstone in Brookside Cemetery in Tecumseh. Even in death, "keeping up with the Joneses" was important for Silvers. *Author photo.*

sell a colt at a discounted rate to saloon keeper Charles Snell. They made a date to meet the next day in the afternoon to perhaps make a deal. Another witness reported hearing crying coming from the Silvers home between 8:00 and 9:00 p.m., with Josephine pleading with her husband to come to her. Though Frank and Josephine did not have a reputation for fighting, the bystander just thought it was a domestic disturbance and did not intervene. Another neighbor, Alice Fitzgerald, stated at the probe that she heard two shots between 9:00 and 10:00 p.m. She did not hear any other gunfire. It was surmised that Frank killed everyone on Saturday night.

The community was shocked by the violence and viewed it as an unsolvable mystery as to why Frank committed this horrendous crime. One vicious rumor spread that Frank killed Josephine because he feared his wife would develop dementia like her mother. There were no reports of any mental decline in his wife, however, and this would not explain why Ada and Edith also had to die. In contrast, there is primary source evidence that I think supports the theory that Frank killed himself and his family to escape from his financial problems. Though he was viewed as very prosperous, at the inquest close friends noted that Frank complained that he was not worth as much as people thought and that he wanted to sell the house in Tecumseh and move his family to his farm. There were rumors that he gambled on horse races, which, if true, certainly would have added to his worries. From a review of the tax records, Frank struggled to pay what was due as early as 1885. His attempt to broker a deal on a horse at a deep discount in the last hours of his life also indicates a person in need of money. I suspect that the financial pressure got to be too much for him, and his pride would not allow him to widely admit that he was in poor economic straits. He had been keeping up appearances for so long and could not bear being a failure and what that would mean for his family. The airing of such an economic reversal would bring shame to the Silverses' good name. Perhaps he thought the only way out for them all was death.

By April 1889, much of the Silvers estate had been settled, except for the house. Even with a greatly reduced price, no one desired to buy the Silverses' home, which now had the reputation of being haunted. It sat empty for years. While several other homes in Tecumseh continue to be viewed as haunted, few today remember the Silvers home, with its arguably more gruesome backstory. So how does one reform a haunted house? One method that seems to have worked in this instance is to remove the home from the scene of the crime. Around 1904, Oscar Packard and his family

After the murder-suicide, the Silverses' home sat empty for several years in Tecumseh. Many whispered that the place was haunted. *Author photo.*

purchased the Silvers house at the greatly reduced price of $300 and moved the home approximately one and a half miles away to Raisin Township in the country. Oscar had a celery farm on that property. The land where the Silverses once lived on South Evans Street is now a parking lot with no tales of it being haunted. Similarly, the former Silver family home, now on its new road, has no stories being circulated about it being haunted either. I believe that this move disrupted the narrative and helped erase the history of this once-haunted house.

CHAPTER 17

THE STACY MANSION AND THE WITCH'S CHAIR

TECUMSEH

Some of the reasons given by ghost hunters as to why earthbound spirits haunt a location often fall into predictable categories in ghost stories, such as the person died violently, or they had unfinished business, or they are a warning to the living of impending doom, or perhaps they just had a strong attachment to the place that they now spook. I think that the specter of the Stacy Mansion in Tecumseh could fit the strong attachment theory. At the time of this writing, the Italianate brick mansion is for sale, and if I had the means, I would love to personally haunt the place. The 7,100-square-foot property includes seven bedrooms, five and a half baths, five fireplaces, a yellow stained-glass window, hardwood floors throughout and a large spiral staircase. I know that if I were an apparition, I would never want to leave such a gorgeous home.

The residence built for Judge Constance Stacy and his family took eight years to complete and originally had twenty-seven rooms. The land on which it sits was reportedly an ancient Native American encampment. Mary Stacy, in an article titled "Reminiscences," related the following in an interview:

> *In 1856–57 during the building of the house, in grading the grounds and ploughing a ditch on the south side of the road for an improvement of the lot and road, was raised a quantity of bones representing a race larger than anyone living here. Physicians were notified to come and see if they were worth saving. Drs. Baldwin, Patterson, Hamilton, and Palmer decided they were worth preserving and took them away with the understanding that they*

> *should put up one skeleton for Mrs. Stacy to put in the garret of the new house when it was finished.*

It is uncertain if Mrs. Stacy ever received and displayed her authentic skeleton in the mansion.

The front of the home was oriented so one could look toward downtown. As could be expected of such a grand home, the Stacy family was very influential and wealthy. Judge Constance Stacy came to Tecumseh from New York in 1836 at nineteen years old with his new bride, Mary. Constance (better known as C.A.) planned to study law. He did become a lawyer and was of service to Tecumseh and the state in a variety of ways over the years. Some of these roles included justice of the peace, judge, newspaper owner and editor, state board of education member, Tecumseh school board member and postmaster. He was instrumental in the development of the Tecumseh business district, Michigan Normal School (now Eastern Michigan University—my alma mater) and the Universalist Church of Tecumseh. C.A. and Mary were the parents of seven children: Scovel, L. Loana, James, Alphonzo, George, Lois and Worthy. Those who survived childhood all became accomplished individuals in their own right. Even with their charmed life, several tragedies befell the Stacys.

C.A. and Mary ended up outliving four of their seven progeny. Two daughters, Lois and Worthy, died while still toddlers. Their son Alphonso died while still a young man due to injuries sustained in a freak train accident. Another son, James, the mayor of Adrian, succumbed to bronchial pneumonia. Both C.A. and Mary took comfort from their Universalist faith to deal with their losses. They celebrated their fiftieth wedding anniversary on August 21, 1888. The *Detroit Free Press* described the elaborate celebration, which had approximately 475 guests:

> *Judge Stacy and his wife still occupy the old homestead at the head of Chicago Street and are enjoying excellent health for people of their age. They endured the ordeal of receiving several hundred guests without any apparent fatigue, and the assembled company seemed to catch the spirit of the occasion. The Judge shook hands with many persons during the day who knew him when he brought his bride from New York and began his domestic life in Tecumseh, half a century ago this month. A golden wedding comes but once in a man's lifetime. The Judge did his part to celebrate the anniversary and his numerous friends reciprocated cheerfully and generously. It was a social event that will be long remembered in Tecumseh.*

This Italianate mansion was built for Judge C.A. Stacy and his family in Tecumseh. Talk persists that the house is troubled by an apparition. *Clara Waldron Historical Room, Tecumseh District Library.*

Unfortunately, C.A. would pass away just shy of two months later. It was no surprise that Mary was grief-stricken. She had an elaborate family plot marker placed in Brookside Cemetery and regularly visited his and other family members' graves until she died in 1905.

The earliest written account that I could uncover indicating the Stacy Mansion was haunted was from 1976. The home had certainly seen better days and had fallen into disrepair. Ann Arbor couple Lee and Michelle Worley purchased the home, and the *Daily Telegram* queried on March 1, "What insanity would lead a young couple to purchase a huge 27-room mansion badly in need of renovation and repair and complete with bats, rats, and ghost stories?" In that same article, Michelle Worley "tells of a young mistress of the house who died in the master bedroom upstairs, and who supposedly haunts the halls even now. At least one Tecumseh resident swears to have seen her ghost coming down the stairs from the bedroom." This wraith in later versions is described as a lady in white and surmised to be Loana. She passed away in the home in 1918 at the age of seventy-three. Perhaps ghosts can appear at whatever age they choose, which would be another perk to being an earthbound spirit.

Over time, the legend expands to include not only the Stacy home but also the Stacy resting place in the Brookside Cemetery. The book *Weird Michigan* describes, "Toward the back of the large cemetery stands a peculiar monument carved from granite in the shape of a comfortable easy chair, known locally as the Witch's Chair. Some have claimed to have photographed spirit orbs near the plot. Engraved on the chair's back is the name of a prominent early family, Stacy." Local Tecumseh residents told the author of *Weird Michigan* that a woman in the family was rumored to be a witch, "or strange or something like that." Such chair-style memorials were not considered peculiar in the nineteenth century; they symbolize the loss of a loved one. These seats also provided a place for the bereaved to sit when they would visit the gravesite. The garden cemetery movement or rural cemetery movement of the mid-nineteenth century encouraged burial grounds with parklike environments to encourage regular visits. Some famous examples in the United States include Mount Auburn in Massachusetts, Laurel Hill in Philadelphia and Lake View Cemetery in Cleveland.

Unfortunately, many modern people are unaware of this history, so some of these chair monuments have gained a nefarious reputation, being referred to as a witch's chair or devil's chair. In most of the variations of this legend, if a person sits in this headstone, they will soon die. These tales are called "legend tripping" by cultural anthropologists and folklorists and involve young people who dare each other to prove their mettle by going to a cursed location, often at night, to test a local legend. Some common types of "legend trips" in the United States include such challenges as visiting an abandoned asylum, haunted tunnel, spooky woods or, in this instance, the graveyard late at night to sit in a "witch's chair." Often these tales have a kernel of truth, but then they become quite fantastical with little supporting historical evidence.

In the legend connected to the Stacys, the Brookside Cemetery chair is claimed to be bewitched by Loana Stacy, even though the monument is a family plot marker. She became saddled with the reputation of a witch as the folktale grew. The book *Weird Michigan* reported, "Perhaps it was Loana's spinsterhood and the family's affiliation with the Universalists that got tongues wagging with the *W* word. Many an outbreak of whooping cough or cases of ailing farm animals were attributed to the supposed powers of the postmaster's daughter." This passage makes it seem like Loana was an odd recluse, but the historical record disputes this view. She was in fact very active in the community. Loana worked at the family newspaper and was a member of the Michigan Woman's Press Association. She was a member of benevolent organizations such as the Order of the Eastern Star and the Women's Relief Corps. Loana was very active in church activities and also volunteered as the clerk for the Universalist church in Tecumseh.

It is accurate that some traditional Protestant faiths held prejudical views of the more liberal Universalist denomination. Yet many of the prominent families in Lenawee County subscribed to this faith, such as the Deweys, Eddys, Fisks and Woodens. This progressive faith, along with Quakerism, was common due to the origins of many of the first settlers to the state. The opening of the Erie Canal in 1825 increased migration to the Michigan Territory, especially from New England. Universalism had its genesis in New England and arrived in Michigan via itinerant preachers in 1829, with societies founded in Pontiac (1830), Adrian (1833) and Ann Arbor (1834). The denomination grew slowly, with only seven churches in the state by 1850, according to the seventh U.S. Census. Universalist beliefs that people are inherently good and capable of perfection were in sympathy with a variety of reform movements, such as temperance, antislavery, universal suffrage and anti–capital punishment. Though it was not considered a mainstream religion, its members were not treated as social pariahs.

Regarding Loana's marital status, it was true that she never married, but spinsterhood did not have the same negative connotations as for earlier generations. Historian Nancy Woloch in the work *Women and the American Experience* illustrated, "Of women born between 1835 and 1855, between 7 and 8 percent never married. In Jane Addam's generation, born 1860 to 1880, between 10 and 11 percent of women never married, and in the next generation, the percentage was only slightly lower. More important, during the late nineteenth century, the spinster, once a marginal member of society, suddenly moved from the periphery of history to the center stage." Loana, like many women who came of age during the Civil War, did not have as many marital prospects, and for college-educated women like herself, the number of appropriate young men was even lower. According to the Michigan Department of Military and Veterans Affairs, "From April 1861 to April 1865, Michigan furnished 90,747 men, not counting 1,982 men commuting and 4,000 Michigan men who served in the units of other states….Of officers serving, 177 were killed, 85 died of wounds, and 96 died of disease. Among the enlisted men, 2,643 were killed, 1,302 died of wounds, and 10,040 died of disease." With approximately 23 percent of the male population of Michigan dead, women who might have married instead entered into professions to support themselves. Upon her father's death in 1888, Loana was appointed postmaster of Tecumseh by President Grover

This burial plot marker for the Stacy family at the Brookside Cemetery in Tecumseh has a myth attached that says if you sit in the chair monument, you will soon die. *Author photo.*

Cleveland. She continued to be active in the community and helped take care of her mother until her death. She had a good reputation in the community, and no primary sources indicate Loana was blamed for misfortunes like epidemics or sickly cows.

My interpretation is that the Stacy Mansion began to be considered haunted when it started to look like a stereotypical spooky house in the 1960s and 1970s. It was severely neglected and rundown. This dilapidation provided a fertile ground for imaginative people to create tales about ghosts, witches and cursed tombs. Luckily, the mansion was given a new lease on life by owners such as the Worleys and saved from destruction. It is arguably the most beautiful home in Tecumseh, whether haunted or not.

CHAPTER 18

TECUMSEH PARK AND INDIAN CROSSING TRAILS PARK

TECUMSEH

When I think of going to a park, I do not usually think of it as a legendary place. Rather, it is a location to enjoy the outdoors, perhaps have a picnic or take a swim. In Tecumseh, however, not one but two such locations have legendary connections. In one instance, at Tecumseh Park, there is a modern tale with little historical basis, and at the other, Indian Crossing Trails Park, a historical location almost became lost to time. To set the scene for the first urban legend, imagine that you decide to go for a hike at Tecumseh Park. The fresh air and exercise will do you and your trusty dog some good, as it is a beautiful day. You walk together past a swimming hole, known by locals as "the pit" since it used to be a gravel pit, where you see some swimmers also enjoying the perfect weather. As you near your destination, your canine freezes and lets out an uncharacteristic low growl. His ears are flat and hackles are raised in fear. At first, you notice a glowing orb floating through the trees. Your gaze follows the orb to the beginning of the woods. There you are surprised to see a young girl about nine years old in a white nightgown holding a teddy bear. You glance briefly at your hound, and when you look back up, the apparition is gone. You decide to forgo the stroll and quickly return home.

According to the tale, this child was kidnapped, murdered and dumped in the woods. She is doomed to forever haunt the location of her demise. The detail of a teddy bear would date the event between 1902 and the present time. However, no such cases have been uncovered that fit the characteristics of this crime. There is no historical support to this tale.

Locally called "the pit" in Tecumseh, this park was formerly a gravel pit. It now features a swimming beach, playground, picnic tables and a shelter house. *Author photo.*

But if one would go online and search for "ghost child with teddy bear," several images pop up. This tale began to be shared online approximately four years ago on the WFMK (East Lansing) radio station's webpage. I surmise that this is a case of people taking outside lore and adapting it to a local location. Many locals in posts have commented that they have never heard this story. It should also be noted that many cross-cultural tales exist that focus on murdered child hauntings.

Aside from this ghostly legend, there are other ancient points of interest in Indian Crossing Trails Park that precede its foundation in 1996, as well as the foundation of Tecumseh itself. The connections to Native American history extend beyond the community being named after the great Shawnee leader. The former owners of the land, Margaret and Chuck Gross, sold the 130-acre property at a loss so that with an $84,000 grant from the Michigan Department of Natural Resources it would be financially feasible to develop the park. There was some controversy that the Native American site—often called the Sacred Circle or Dancing Ground, the location of which had been lost to time—might be uncovered by establishing Indian Crossing Trails. An early mention of this land dates from 1879 in the *History and Biographical Record of Lenawee County, Michigan*:

> *It was laid out in the form of a square and a circle, with an opening from the one to the other, where they joined—the trails all leading to and from the circle; and both parts having an embankment of about four feet in height, and having in the center of the circular part, a pit of five or six feet deep. By digging in the bottom of this pit, nothing special was found, except some charcoal or charred wood. When the white settlers first came here, there were some cedar posts in the outer embankment, and there were evidences of the place being quite often used for meetings or gatherings of some kind. But the Indians always seemed reluctant to say anything about the objects for which it was used; and whether for war dances, or worship, or some ceremonies of medicine men, it would be difficult to tell or guess. It was generally spoken of by the early settlers, as the Indian dancing ground—some thought it might be the burial place of some chief, but this was all a matter of mere conjecture or surmise.*

The Tecumseh Parks and Recreation Department stressed that they had no plans to rediscover the location of the Sacred Circle or any other possible Native American locations on the property to protect the integrity of the site and dissuade artifact hunters. Yet this policy was reversed in 2014, and some of the early critics changed their mind, concerned that the site might be lost forever. Samuel Anderson, for his Eagle Scout project, uncovered the location of the Dancing Ground and had a sign installed indicating its location. This display reads, "Early historians of Tecumseh have written that this area was a main crossroads of Native American travel where two ancient trails once met. At this spot where two trails crossed was an earthwork created around 1,000 A.D. by the Mound Builder or Hopewell culture. Early settlers referred to the area as 'Indian Dancing Ground' or 'Council Grounds.' In 1832 the circle and square earthwork were destroyed when plans for the Globe Mill called for a sawmill to be built at this location." The Globe Mill operated until 1858. The *Tecumseh Herald* quoted the seventeen-year-old high school senior: "This area was a magnet for all of the Indians in southeast Michigan, northwest Ohio and northeast Indiana. They used to meet twice a year at this site. It was a very important part of their culture."

This location was certainly significant to the Great Lakes region. Circular dance grounds of Native Americans remained common in the Upper Great Lakes region throughout the eighteenth and nineteenth centuries. Dance and music could serve a celebratory function but also a sacred purpose for Native Americans. Ceremonial dances in the Great Lakes region included those for protection, healing, thanksgiving and supplication. Local journalist Mickey Alvarado wondered if the Sacred Circle in Tecumseh might have been a solstice location, such as other more well-known sites like Cahokia, Fort Ancient or Chaco Canyon. Alvarado reported:

> *I'd waited months for the summer solstice to return, as the longest day of the year would help prove or denounce my unsupported suspicions of finding a Native American solstice marker within our midst. The solstice morning arrived and it was perfect, giving a clear view of a beautiful sunrise. When the sun's beams crested the top of a nearby bluff they passed over the solstice rock and directly over a large marker stone, some 75 or so yards away. I'm not a scientist or archaeologist, but even I could tell it was more than a mere coincidence. Another phenomenon occurred as well. Call me crazy if you will, but I saw it. When the sun first burst over the top of the bluff it created a path of light that ran from the south to the north, forming a shape of a slithering serpent. Its bright path first appeared on Raisin River and slowly moved to the main Indian trail heading north. As the sun pushed higher into the sky the snake of light wriggled up the steep bluff and eventually disappeared with the mist into a portal created by a solstice-marking boulder.*

Many Native American groups did observe the summer and winter solstices as times of renewal with ceremonies. Associate professor of environmental studies Rosalyn LaPie described, "The winter solstice is the day of the year when the Northern Hemisphere has the fewest hours of sunlight and the Southern Hemisphere has the most. For indigenous peoples, it has been a time to honor their ancient sun deity. They passed their knowledge down to successive generations through complex stories and ritual practices." Dozens of cultures constructed sites based on the sun's position. Unfortunately, according to anthropologists Howey and Burg, it is often difficult to determine how the ceremonial earthworks located in the Great Lakes were used by these early civilizations. In their article "Landscape Bundling of Ceremonial Earthworks," they summarized:

> *While it is well-recognized that the monuments constructed by small-scale societies are almost always ceremonial in nature, these frameworks reduce ritual to the transactional, existing only to facilitate another purpose—be it social integration, evolutionary cooperation, or signaling. Interpreting the ritual nature of monuments as existing to facilitate some other goal denies the distinct possibility that for the people who built them, the ritual nature of these monuments was their purpose. Indeed, the ontologies of many non-western societies do not differentiate between ritual life and daily life, nature and culture, or animate and inanimate things.*

The location of the Sacred Circle does indicate that it was a circular enclosure and not a burial site. Howey has completed extensive mapping on Native American constructions, primarily of the Late Precontact era (1000–1600 CE). "These enclosures became these shared ritual spaces. They were on rivers so they were accessible to multiple groups," says Howey, adding that canoe travel along Michigan's major rivers enabled the ancestral Anishinaabeg people to transport themselves and their goods long distances. What is perhaps most amazing about the Sacred Circle in Tecumseh is that we know its former location at all, as Howey estimates up to 80 percent of these places were destroyed over time.

A final point of interest near the Standish Dam is a memorial stone dedicated to the white deer of Tecumseh. In 2004, a rare albino deer was spotted in the area of the park. It is estimated that only one in thirty thousand deer will be born with this condition. Many cultures, including Native American nations, believe a white deer to be sacred and a symbol of the divine. The white deer of Tecumseh lived several years in the wild,

This memorial at Indian Crossing Trails Park in Tecumseh is dedicated to a white deer that once roamed the area. A white deer is a lucky sign in many cultures. *Author photo.*

which is also uncommon for albinos. Unfortunately, it was struck by a car and perished. Several people came together, including the Leh Nah Weh Native American Organization, and held a sacred burial ceremony for this unusual animal. The marker notes, "She roamed free and captured our hearts."

CHAPTER 19
HAMILTON HOUSE

TECUMSEH

Perhaps the most atypical haunted house in Tecumseh, to my mind, is the Hamilton House. This modified Greek Revival home was built by twin brothers Elisha and Elijah Anderson, circa 1840. The Anderson brothers were master craftsmen and constructed several of the impressive structures of early Tecumseh, including another home directly across from the Hamilton House, also in a Greek Revival style. Rumors persist that an underground tunnel once connected the two homes in order to assist the brothers in their abolitionist work. Dr. Increase Hamilton came to Tecumseh to practice medicine in 1844 and purchased the home that now bears his name.

A variety of unusual phenomena has been reported at this abode by several former residents. Some incidents include lights that flicker on and off, ghostly footsteps unconnected to any human being heard in the vicinity of the attic and books that fly off the shelves in the middle of the night. Perhaps most frightening to me is that previous owners Lance and Cindy Tennant were forced to flee and eventually abandon their home due to an infestation of bats. In addition, another former owner, Margaret Gross, always kept the basement door securely latched in her property. She explained, "We heard scratching noises from the other side like a dog is at the door." The Grosses noted that an ice pick was mounted above said door when they moved in, like it was at the ready in case something would break through the portal. Paranormal investigator Jeff Westover made a visit to the property

This Greek Revival home in Tecumseh was designed by twin brothers Elisha and Elijah Anderson, as was a house across the street. *Clara Waldron Historical Room, Tecumseh District Library.*

approximately five years ago and found his experience at the house more than chilling:

> *I went in for two different investigations. I like fine art photography and one of my specialties is haunted locations, but while I'm doing that I like to record audio, almost like interviewing a house, and I try to learn as much as I can about a historical location. I'll ask questions of a historical nature trying to get proper answers. While I was in the basement I had a woman's voice record clearly, "You're not welcome." I didn't hear it, but I recorded it, and I recorded a lot of voices in the basement. It's funny when*

This spooky photo, taken by Jeff Westover, was captured in the Hamilton House of Tecumseh. *Clara Waldron Historical Room, Tecumseh District Library.*

> *that happened because even though I didn't hear it, I didn't feel welcome at the time. I could've stayed overnight in that house for two weeks, and I didn't go back after that.*

What is particularly unusual about this haunting is that there is no narrative indicating why the property is so active. No major tragedies are connected to the home. Though the Grosses jokingly called their ghost Dr. Hamilton, there is no conclusive evidence to indicate he is the spirit or spirits, as the case may be. Dr. Increase Hamilton had a good reputation and was a beloved family doctor. He served on the Board of Trustees of Kalamazoo College. He was active in Republican politics. Hamilton was also an engaged member of the Baptist faith. He was widowed twice and fathered four children. It is true that some people died in the home over the years, such as Hamilton's second wife, Harriet, in 1872, but this was commonplace in the nineteenth century. There were no stories after Dr. Hamilton's death of unusual happenings in the home. There was nothing nefarious about the ways that people have passed away in the home. For example, C.H. Williamson, a businessman and grocery store owner who lived in this house for several years, died following an illness in 1938. It appears that the paranormal stories reported about the home did not surface until the later part of the twentieth century.

The Hamilton House was severely damaged by a chimney fire in 1965, which destroyed the downstairs parlor and music room. One working theory published by the *Tecumseh Herald* as to why the property became viewed as haunted is due to a period in the late twentieth century when there were a series of revolving owners and the Hamilton House seemed to be always back on the real estate market. Rumors began to spread as to what could possibly be wrong with the place. This might explain the historical origins of this haunting, but it does not shine a light on why so many former owners report unusual occurrences on the property. That mystery still remains.

CHAPTER 20
THE MAGNETIC MANSION
TIPTON

There are several instances from classic literature in which an actual property inspires a fictional story, such as *The House of Seven Gables*, *Wuthering Heights* and *The Great Gatsby*. Similarly, a home in Tipton, Michigan, served as the muse for the novel *Magnetic Mansion: Return to Eden*. The author of this work, Forrest Haskell Jr. (1936–2023), lived in this impressive Tudor Revival–style mansion, located near Jefferey Lake and Evans Lake in the Irish Hills, in the 1960s. The hero of *Magnetic Mansion* (2007) is Zachary Heikel, a thinly disguised version of Haskell, as many biographical events from his life are contained in the book.

Haskell was born in Detroit, attended Northwestern High School and was drafted into the army. Following his military service, he married Nancy Joann, and they raised four children together. Haskell had several successful business enterprises. After he retired, Haskell moved to Texas and began to write books. He would self-publish six works; most are now out of print. Three of them—*The Magnetic Mansion*, *Second Genesis* and *Return to* Zion—referenced the home in Tipton, so it made a lasting impression on him. Haskell promoted his book *Magnetic Mansion* as based on a baffling true story.

That claim of a true story is highly unlikely, as this poor work of fiction includes a multitude of fantastical situations, each more absurd than the last. The basic plot is that Heikel buys a rundown mansion to renovate and uncovers, with his wife and four children, a series of mysteries and supernatural experiences connected to the home. To his credit, Haskell did incorporate some of the legends and historical aspects of the property

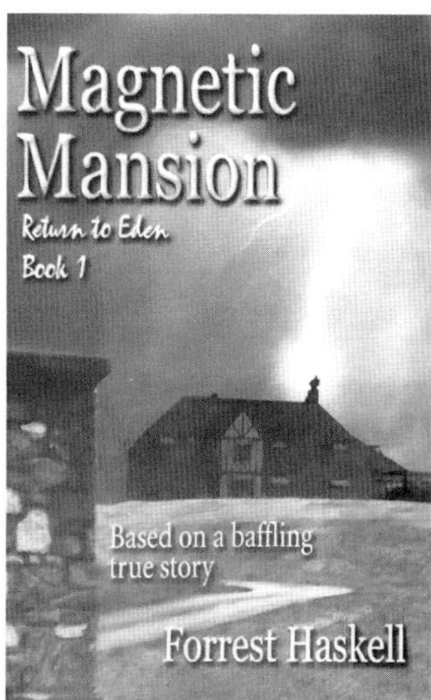

This is an image of one of the fantastical books written by Forrest Haskell, inspired by the home he once lived in in the Irish Hills. *Author's collection.*

in his novel. For example, the home was constructed for a wealthy man. In 1931, Charles Breyman (1866–1945) of Toledo, Ohio, a very successful dredging contractor, had this home built as a summer place. The Tudor Revival style of this house was popular in the United States from 1890 to 1940, with its use of round door arches, partially timbered façades, massive fireplaces, multipane window glazing and a steep roof. Most of the year, the Breyman family lived in the exclusive Old West End of Toledo. That Colonial Revival home, built in 1912 for the Breymans, was designed by the architect George Rheinfrank with four bedrooms and one and a half baths. In the novel, a wealthy man had the mansion built as well, but in this instance, he was a corrupt member of the Detroit bench, Judge Levison, who worked with the Purple Gang.

The Purple Gang, also called the Sugar House Gang, was a notorious group of Jewish mobsters headquartered near the northwest side of Detroit during the 1920s–'30s at the height of Prohibition. Initially in the 1910s, they were just a small group of teenagers involved in petty theft and protection rackets, but the organization would grow to fifty members with involvement in kidnapping, alcohol trafficking, bootlegging, armed robbery and murder. The main leaders of the gang were the Bernstein brothers: Abe, Joseph, Isadore "Izzy" and Raymond. The origin of their nickname is uncertain. One popular explanation is that two shopkeepers were talking about the young hoodlums and one noted, "These boys are not like other children of their age; they're tainted, off color." "Yes," replied the other shopkeeper. "They're rotten, purple like the color of bad meat. They're a Purple Gang."

Given the gang's involvement in the illegal alcohol trade, there are stories of the Purples traveling U.S. 12 between Detroit and Chicago regularly. As an aside, I once looked at a lake property off the Chicago road for sale that had an old rusted-out Model T in the bushes near the road. The realtor stated that members of the Purple Gang crashed the Ford when they were being pursued by the police. As a history buff, I may have been more inclined to buy the place if there had been better documentation of this.

The decline of this syndicate began with infighting and ended with its top leadership behind bars after the Collingwood Manor Massacre. The Detroit Historical Society summarized this event:

> *Ray Bernstein, a key Purple Gang leader, arranged for the death of the Little Jewish Navy leaders Joe Lebowitz, Hymie Paul, and Isadore Sutker. On September 16, 1931, the three men, escorted by Sol Levine, went to meet with the Purple Gang at Apartment 211 at 1740 Collingwood Avenue. They were told it was a friendly meeting. Instead, Purple Gang gunmen Harry Keywell and Irving Milberg murdered Lebowitz, Paul, and Sutker when they arrived. Levine was spared due to his friendship with Bernstein. Fearing that he would be targeted by the Purple Gang, Levine testified against the gang during the subsequent murder trial. Bernstein, Keywell, and Milberg were sentenced to life imprisonment. The Collingwood Manor Massacre crippled the Purple Gang's influence by leading to the arrests of vital members. Intra-gang rivalries, inter-gang disputes, legal convictions, and multiple homicides weakened the group. Other criminal organizations filled the voids left by the Purple Gang's dismantled empire.*

Rumors persist that the Purple Gang hung out at the Magnetic Mansion in the past, yet there is no supporting evidence to corroborate this tale or that any horrible events took place at this home. Additionally, the timing is a bit off in that the Magnetic Mansion was built in 1931, the same year the gang was focused on its legal woes. Another legend that Al Capone slept at the home is also suspect since Capone was convicted of tax evasion in 1931. Capone served time until 1939, when he was released to a hospital due to his failing health. Prohibition ended in 1933 nationwide, thus shifting the business model for organized crime away from rumrunning and bootlegging.

In the 1940s, Cyrus Camp purchased the property and promoted it as a lake rental. In the 1960s, as noted previously, the Haskell family lived at the four-bedroom, 5,038-square-foot home. Following the residence of the Haskells, the house would have several more owners and fall into severe disrepair. As we have seen, an abandoned, dilapidated house is almost bound to develop rumors of ghosts. Haskell's book likely encouraged other legends, such as that a secret society built it, that money was hidden in the home, that bodies were buried on the property, that a submerged armored car was in the lake and that tainted water drove residents insane. Another major premise of the novel was that unusual magnetic forces were on this land. Haskell noted that similar effects were present at the nearby Irish Hill tourist

Mystery hills and mystery spots are tourist attractions that exist along roadsides all over the United States. Michigan has a few, including this one in Onsted. *Author photo.*

attraction Mystery Hill. There are many of these types of funhouses across the United States, where the claim is that the laws of gravity and physics are defied, yet in actuality, this phenomenon is created through optical illusions and unlevel building practices. According to the Roadside America website, the oldest example still in operation is the Oregon Vortex (1930) near Gold Hill. The Mystery Hill in the Irish Hills dates to 1952.

Even with the rumor and poor state of the Magnetic Mansion, Ken and Amy Adams purchased the foreclosed home in 2010. The *Daily Telegram* reported on the state of the property: "Windows were broken. A tree and brush grew in the long-empty pool. The roof was in danger of collapsing in one spot. Poison ivy vines ran up to the chimney. Bats, birds, and wasps lived in the house. When Ken first saw the place, there was a bird flying around in one bedroom and water was cascading down the staircase." During the yearlong reconstruction by Ypsilanti Renovations, only an old empty safe and a hidden compartment were discovered by the crew.

The Adamses were told by Haskell that he had seen strange images reflected in mirrors. However, it would have been in Haskell's interest to promote the mansion as a supernatural place. The Adamses did not have any paranormal experiences themselves. On August 19, 2010, the SouthEast Michigan Ghost Hunters Society investigated the property. This group was founded in 1996 and is one of the oldest in the state. From reviewing their Facebook posts of this examination, they did not believe the place to be haunted. They thought it was just a ruined mansion. As an aside, I find it refreshing that these paranormal investigators have the integrity to call it as they see it when I have found too many ghost hunters who think every old place is haunted. It seems that with the renovations of the Magnetic Mansion, much of its spooky reputation has dissipated, and it is once again viewed by most as it was designed to be: simply a charming lake house.

BIBLIOGRAPHY

Primary Sources

Battle Creek Enquirer. "Boulder and Bronze Tablet, Gift of Battle Creek Man, Dedicated." August 18, 1931.

———. "Hudson Banker Dies." April 16, 1926.

———. "Participate in Unique Service." May 29, 1925.

———. "Plan Indian Burial." May 20, 1925.

Bingham, Stephen. *Early History of Michigan with Biographies of State Officers, Members of Congress, Judges, and Legislators*. Thorp and Godfrey, 1888.

Bryan Democrat. "The Execution of John Cowell." August 24, 1865.

Cass County Republican. "A Family Frozen to Death." January 14, 1864.

Cleveland Daily Leader. "Further of the Treadwell Murder." September 3, 1864.

Combination Atlas Map of Lenawee County: 1874, 1893, 1916. Everts & Stewart, 1916.

Daily Ohio Statesman. "Murder and Robbery: A Strange Lawsuit." September 24, 1868.

Daily Telegram. "Blissfield-Based Ghosthunting Group Looks for Paranormal Activity." October 26, 2013.

———. "The Ghosts Among Us." October 31, 1977.

———. "Hudson Boy Drowns in a Pool on Lawn." August 14, 1942.

———. "Martin L. Gay Dies of a Heart Attack." September 2, 1943.

———. "Morenci." February 9, 1944.

———. "New Clinton Inn Owners Want to Be Part of the Community." June 10, 2019.

———. "120-Year-Old Tecumseh Home Restored by Ann Arbor Couple." March 1, 1976.

———. "Report Issued on Devils Lake Crash." July 30, 1971.

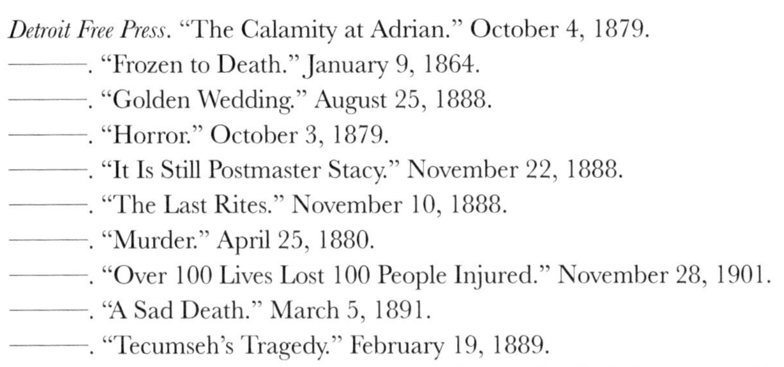

Detroit Free Press. "The Calamity at Adrian." October 4, 1879.

———. "Frozen to Death." January 9, 1864.

———. "Golden Wedding." August 25, 1888.

———. "Horror." October 3, 1879.

———. "It Is Still Postmaster Stacy." November 22, 1888.

———. "The Last Rites." November 10, 1888.

———. "Murder." April 25, 1880.

———. "Over 100 Lives Lost 100 People Injured." November 28, 1901.

———. "A Sad Death." March 5, 1891.

———. "Tecumseh's Tragedy." February 19, 1889.

Dewey, Franklin. "Address at the Farmers' Picnic, Devils Lake, August 22, 1883." Central Michigan University. www.cmich.edu/docs/default-source/academic-affairs-division/libraries/clarke-historical-library/explore-online/native-american-materials/excerpts-and-annotations/20211011_nativeamericanmaterials_dewey-_f_a_pg_536-542_033e767c160-70f5-4be3-9aa9-cad92cc644a3.pdf?sfvrsn=3f7373df_6.

———. *Dewey Cambridge History: A Collection of Historical Articles*. Lenawee Historical Society.

Forest and Stream 61. "Memories of Fishing at Devil's Lake Michigan." (1903): 107–8.

Hogaboam, James. *The Bean Creek Valley*. Jas. M. Scarritt, 1876.

Huron Shore Tourist Association. "Get Acquainted." *The Ohio Motorist* 15 (July 1923): 41.

Ironwood Daily Globe. "Steam Shovel Digs Up Skeletons of Indians." November 20, 1923.

Lathrop, Elise. *Early American Inns and Taverns*. Robert McBride & Company, 1926.

Mahan, Asa. *Autobiography, Intellectual, Moral, and Spiritual*. T. Woolmer, 1882.

Michigan Bankers Association. *The Michigan Banker*. Vol. 22. University of Illinois at Urbana-Champaign, 1925.

Michigan County Histories and Atlases. "Siam School." University of Michigan Library Digital Collections. name.umdl.umich.edu/m/micounty/3116971.0001.001.

Michigan Department of Public Instruction. *Sixty-First Annual Report of the Superintendent of Public Instruction*. Robert Smith Printing Company, 1898.

Michigan State Teachers' Association. *The Michigan Journal of Education and Teachers' Magazine*. Vol. 3. Henry Barnes, 1856.

MLive.com. "Historic Hewitt House Renovated, Walker Tavern Due Up Next." August 5, 2016. www.mlive.com/news/jackson/2016/08/historic_hewitt_house_renovate.html.

News-Messenger. "Personal Experience Leads to Fascination with the Paranormal." October 21, 2009.

"Notices." *Federal Register* 83 (July 12, 2018). Authenticated U.S. Government Information. www.govinfo.gov/content/pkg/FR-2018-07-12/pdf/2018-14935.pdf.

Portrait and Biographical Album: Lenawee County, Michigan. Chapman Brothers, 1888.

Sloan, Samuel. *The Model Architect*. E.S. Jones & Company, 1852.

Smith, Lydia. *Behind the Scenes, Or Life in an Insane Asylum*. Culver, Page, Hoyne, & Co., 1878.

Tecumseh Herald. "4-Year Project Nears End." March 26, 1992.

———. "Ghostbusting Scares Up Spooky Tales." October 30, 1986.

———. "Sacred Sites Lost, but Not Forgotten." November 7, 2002.

True Northerner. "Verdict of Manslaughter." October 17, 1879.

True Republican. "Killed Himself." March 7, 1891.

Tuttle, Charles. *General History of the State of Michigan*. R.D.S. Tyler & Company, 1873.

Whitney, W.A., and R.I. Bonner. *History and Biographical Record of Lenawee County, Michigan*. W. Stearns & Company, 1879.

Secondary Sources

Alexander-Bloch, Benjamin. "1901 Wreck's Horrifying Story Is Still Potent." *The Blade*, March 19, 2007. www.toledoblade.com/frontpage/2007/03/19/1901-wreck-s-horrific-story-is-still-potent.html.

Alvarado, Mickey. "Some Things Shouldn't Be Exposed." *Tecumseh Herald*, June 25, 2008.

Association of American Railroads. "All Aboard the Ghost Train." www.aar.org/article/ghost-train.

Bachanov, Arlene. "Croswell: 150 Years Old and Improved." *Lenawee Neighbors*, May–June 2017.

———. "Renovating an Evans Lake Home Reveals Tales of Ghosts and Mobsters." *Daily Telegram*, March 14, 2011.

———. "Tours Share Tales of Croswell Hauntings." *Daily Telegram*, October 21, 2007.

The Best of the Brooklyn Exponent Attic: An Historical Look at the Greater Irish Hills Area. Brooklyn Exponent, 2006.

Brighton, Margaret. *Lake Reflections: Chronicles of Devils and Round Lakes*. Lakes Preservation League, 1996.

Bullard, Loring. *Healing Waters: Missouri's Historic Mineral Springs and Spas*. University of Missouri Press, 2004.

Cherry, Dan. *Along the Trails of Michemanetue*. Dan Cherry, 2009.

———. "Devils Hole Became One of Devil's Lake Earliest Stories of Legend." *Daily Telegram*, April 26, 2022.

———. "Lenawee School District Consolidation Over the Years." *Daily Telegram*, March 26, 2019.

———. "1965 Palm Sunday Tornado Remembered by Residents." *Daily Telegram*, April 11, 2015.

Clarke Historical Library, Central Michigan University. "The Potawatomi Experience of Federal Removal Policy." www.cmich.edu/research/clarke-historical-library/explore-collection/explore-online/native-american-material/native-american-treaty-rights/historical-issues/the-potawatomi-experience-of-federal-removal-policy#:~:text=Removal%2C%201833,Creek%20Reservation%20in%20eastern%20Kansas.

"Clinton Inn History." The Clinton Inn. theclintoninn.com/history.

DeGraaf, Kenneth. "A Haunting at the Heights." Spectra, October 30, 2015. www.shuspectra.com/2450/news/a-haunting-at-the-heights.

Department of Military and Veterans Affairs. "The Civil War." www.michigan.gov/dmva/about/history/military-events/highlights/the-civil-war#:~:text=Michigan's%20Contribution&text=According%20to%20official%20regimental%20commander's,and%2010%2C040%20died%20of%20disease.

Detroit Historical Society. "Purple Gang." detroithistorical.org/learn/encyclopedia-of-detroit/purple-gang.

Dunbar, Willis, and George May. *Michigan: A History of the Wolverine State*. W.B. Eerdmans Publishing Company, 1995.

Frazier, Don. "A Spectacular, Tragic Storm." *Daily Telegram*, February 10, 1976.

Frost, Julieanna. *Adrian*. Images of America. Arcadia Publishing, 2011.

Frownfelder, Dave. "Tecumseh Boy Restores Historic Native American Site." *Tecumseh Herald*, November 17, 2014.

Gable, Erik. *Behind the Curtain: 150 Years at Michigan's Oldest Theater*. Croswell Opera House and Fine Arts Association, 2016.

Gavrilovich, Peter, and Bill McGraw. *The Detroit Almanac*. Detroit Free Press, 2000.

Ghosts of America. "Ghost Sightings." www.ghostsofamerica.com.

Godfrey, Linda. *Weird Michigan: Your Travel Guide to Michigan's Local Legends and Best Kept Secrets*. Stirling Publishing Company, 2006.

Hamlin Church, Jennifer. *Hail, Siena! Siena Heights University: The First Hundred Years*. Siena Heights University, 2019.

Haskell, Forrest. *Magnetic Mansion: Return to Eden, Book 1*. Top Publications, 2007.

Haughton, Brian. *Famous Ghost Stories: Legends and Lore*. Rosen Publishing Group, 2012.

Heineman, Brad. "Morenci's Historic Rex Theatre Sees New Life After Owner Revitalizes Structure." *Daily Telegram*, December 11, 2011.

Howey, Meghan, and Marieka Brouwer Burg. "Landscape Bundling of Ceremonial Earthworks: Incorporating Ethnohistoric and Contemporary

Indigenous Ontologies to Revive Great Lakes Archaeological Legacy Datasets." *Journal of Anthropological Anthropology* 62 (June 2021). www.sciencedirect.com/science/article/abs/pii/S0278416521000052.

Huhman, Lonnie. "1901 'Wreck of the Wabash' Burial Site Located." *Daily Telegram*, January 13, 2016.

Jackson, Tarryl. "Devils Lake Restaurant Reopens with New Name 18 Months After the Fire." MLive, June 29, 2011. www.mlive.com/business/jackson-lansing/2011/06/devils_lake_restaurant_reopens.html.

Kim, Juliana. "U.S. Pedestrian Deaths Reach a 40-Year High." NPR. June 28, 2023. www.npr.org/2023/06/26/1184034017/us-pedestrian-deaths-high-traffic-car.

Kuipers, Kern, and Amanda Payeur. *Tecumseh: The First Century*. Arcadia Publishing, 2006.

LaPier, Rosalyn. "What Winter Solstice Rituals Tell Us About Indigenous People." The Conversation. theconversation.com/what-winter-solstice-rituals-tell-us-about-indigenous-people-108327.

Lennard, Ray, and Don Cherry. *Yesterday and Today at Devil's Lake*. W.G. Thompson House Museum, 2011.

Lindquist, Charles. *Adrian: The City That Worked*. Lenawee County Historical Society, 2004.

Meyer, Zlati. "Michigan's Fearsome Dogman." *Detroit Free Press*, October 31, 2011.

Michigan Department of Education. "Michigan Legislative Biography." mdoe.state.mi.us/legislators/Legislator/LegislatorDetail/1866.

Milan, Jon, and Gail Offen. *Michigan Haunts: Public Places, Eerie Spaces*. Arcadia Publishing, 2019.

Milwaukee Public Museum. "Potawatomi Culture." www.mpm.edu/content/wirp/ICW-56.

Our Journey in Time: Morenci, Michigan 1833–1976. Morenci Bicentennial Committee, 1976.

Potier, Beth. "Michigan's Mystery Monuments." UNH Today, July 19, 2016. www.unh.edu/unhtoday/2016/07/michigans-mystery-monuments.

Proctor, Diane. *Beyond the Boulevard. Tecumseh: Historic Buildings of Tecumseh, Michigan.* Tecumseh Area Historical Society, 1996.

RoadsideAmerica. "Mystery Spots." www.roadsideamerica.com/story/29062#google_vignette.

Roys, Barbara. *Ho! For Devils Lake*. Exponent Press, 1998.

Rubenstein, Bruce, and Lawrence Ziewacz. *Michigan: A History of the Great Lakes State*. Harlan Davidson, 2002.

Ryan, Mary Philip. *Amid the Alien Corn*. Jones Wood Press, 1967.

Savage McAlester, Virginia. *A Field Guide to American Houses*. Knopf, 1984.

Sheckler Finch, Jackie. *Michigan Off the Beaten Path*. Globe Pequot, 2021.

Smith, Leanne. "Peak Through Time: From Grueling Stagecoach Travel to Tale of 'Murder Room' Walker Tavern Has It All." MLive, October 8, 2014. www.mlive.com/news/jackson/2014/10/peek_through_time_from_gruelin.html.

Smith, Patti. *Michigan Beer: A Heady History*. The History Press, 2022.

TLCPL Architecture. "Architecture of Northwest Ohio." tlcplarchitecture.omeka.net.

Vassar, Shea. "Digging Up the Indian Burial Ground Trope." Film School Rejects. filmschoolrejects.com/indian-burial-ground-trope.

Vogel, Virgil. *Indian Names in Michigan*. University of Michigan Press, 1986.

Watts, Linda. *Encyclopedia of American Folklore*. Facts on File, 2007.

Weible, Susanne. "Leoni Was Home to a Bustling College." MLive, September 10, 2007. www.mlive.com/citpat_history/2007/09/leoni_was_home_to_bustling_col.html.

Wessel, Bob. "The Evolution of Lenawee County's Civil Townships." *Daily Telegram*, September 3, 2020.

———. "Tales of Lenawee County's Spirits and Hauntings Through the Years." *Daily Telegram*, October 26, 2021.

Westover, Jeff. "Ghost Highway Photography." *Ghost Highway*. ghosthighway.wordpress.com.

Woodward, Frank. *The Early History of Clintonites*. Historical Society of Clinton, 2006.

Ypsilanti Restoration. "The Magnetic Mansion." www.ypsilantirestoration.com/IrishHills1.htm.

About the Author

Julieanna Frost has been a writer and educator for over twenty-five years. Her main research areas include women's history, religious studies and American culture. She received her doctorate degree from the Union Institute and University in 2007 with a specialization in women's history. Dr. Frost has presented extensively nationally and internationally. She has several publications to her name, including the books *Teaching the Pure Lutheran Gospel: The Life of Rosa Young*; *Adrian* (Images of America); *The Worthy Virgins: Mary Purnell and Her City of David*; *Chemo Fashion Fridays: One Woman's Breast Cancer Journey*; and *The Green Scriptures*. She is the recipient of several honors and awards. Dr. Frost is an active member of the Communal Studies Association. She also loves reading a good ghost story when not researching the past.